face to face

DISCOVER HOW MENTORING

CAN CHANGE YOUR LIFE

JAYME HULL with Laura Captari

MOODY PUBLISHERS

CHICAGO

All Scripture quotations, unless otherwise indicated, are taken from the Holy Bible, New International Version®, NIV®. Copyright © 1973, 1978, 1984, 2011 by Biblica, Inc.™ Used by permission of Zondervan. All rights reserved worldwide. www.zondervan.com. The "NIV" and "New International Version" are trademarks registered in the United States Patent and Trademark Office by Biblica, Inc.™

Scripture quotations marked ESV are from The Holy Bible, English Standard Version® (ESV®), copyright © 2001 by Crossway, a publishing ministry of Good News Publishers. Used by permission. All rights reserved.

Scripture quotations marked (NLT) are taken from the Holy Bible, New Living Translation, copyright © 1996, 2004, 2007, 2013 by Tyndale House Foundation. Used by permission of Tyndale House Publishers, Inc., Carol Stream, Illinois 60188. All rights reserved.

Scripture quotations marked THE MESSAGE or MSG are from The Message, copyright © by Eugene H. Peterson 1993, 1994, 1995, 1996, 2000, 2001, 2002. Used by permission of Tyndale House Publishers, Inc.

Scripture quotations marked NASB are taken from the New American Standard Bible®, Copyright © 1960, 1962, 1963, 1968, 1971, 1972, 1973, 1975, 1977, 1995 by The Lockman Foundation. Used by permission. (www.Lockman.org)

Edited by Pam Pugh   Cover design: Connie Gabbert Design and Illustration
Interior design: Ragont Design   Illustration/lettering by Connie Gabbert
Textured background cover image copyright © by foxie/Shutterstock (115826617).
All rights reserved.
Author photo: Lindey Newton

Library of Congress Cataloging-in-Publication Data

Names: Hull, Jayme.
Title: Face to face : discover how mentoring can change your life / Jayme Hull, with Laura Captari.
Description: Chicago : Moody Publishers, 2016. | Includes bibliographical references.
Identifiers: LCCN 2015039299 | ISBN 9780802413826
Subjects: LCSH: Christian women—Religious life. | Mentoring—Religious aspects—Christianity.
Classification: LCC BV4527 .H849 2016 | DDC 206/.1—dc23 LC record available at http://lccn.loc.gov/2015039299

We hope you enjoy this book from Moody Publishers. Our goal is to provide high-quality, thought-provoking books and products that connect truth to your real needs and challenges. For more information on other books and products written and produced from a biblical perspective, go to www.moodypublishers.com or write to:

Moody Publishers
820 N. LaSalle Boulevard
Chicago, IL 60610

1 3 5 7 9 10 8 6 4 2

Printed in the United States of America

Praise for *Face to Face*

Jayme Hull is an amazing woman who practices what she preaches, and it has been my absolute delight to mentor her over the past year as she's been preparing to release the phenomenal book you hold in your hands. When you get to know Jayme, you'll understand how passionate she is about having a mentor, and being a mentor. I believe *Face to Face* is not just a ministry but a movement that will equip the body of Christ to more effectively pass the baton of faith from one generation to the next!

—SHANNON ETHRIDGE, author, Every Woman's Battle series and founder of the B.L.A.S.T. Mentoring Program (Building Leaders, Authors, Speakers & Teachers)

Years ago, Jayme Hull walked and prayed with me through some of the toughest years of my life. She took me under her wing and began teaching me how to apply God's Word to my daily life. *Face to Face* is a beautifully written guide that teaches both mentors and mentees how to take the journey together to find purpose and understanding through Jesus Christ. This book is so real and uplifting and it will stay by my bedside for years to come.

—NATALIE HEMBY, Nashville songwriter

Life is complicated and often difficult. Too many people are filling their lives with regrets and "if onlys." But it doesn't have to be that way! In her book *Face to Face,* Jayme Hull demonstrates how people can prosper from the wisdom, encouragement, and counsel of others along their journey. Brimming with wisdom, this book will inform, encourage, and inspire you!

—RICHARD BLACKABY, coauthor, *Experiencing God*

One of the most pressing needs of this generation is for strong mentoring relationships. In the Scriptures, there was Elijah and Elisha, Naomi and Ruth, Paul and Timothy, and—most importantly—the Lord Jesus Christ and His faithful disciples. Jayme Hull has written a spiritual and practical guide to developing a heart and game plan for mentoring others. You will be tremendously encouraged and blessed by this anointed book *Face to Face*.

—ELLEN OLFORD, director of women's ministries at Central Church, Memphis, TN

Face to Face is an essential tool for the journey of mentor relationships for both the mentee *and* mentor. It walks you through hard steps that come in life, guiding the best way to find, embrace, learn, and grow from a mentor. The author provides important reminders that God is the foundation on which those relationships stand.

—TAMARA MOORE, millennial business professional

To my husband, John:
You are my lifelong love, companion, and friend.
And to our children, Joanna (and Skylar),
Jason (and Sarah), and Jered (and Lauren):
You are my inspiration for mentoring
and the hope of the next generation.
—JAYME

To my mentors:
Thank you for challenging me to step into new spaces.
Thank you for showing up authentically when
I needed you most. You've given me courage
to dare greatly, and I'm never looking back.
—LAURA

And to you, the reader:
May you be brave enough to be
vulnerable, strong enough to reach out,
and may you meet God in new ways
as you connect with your mentor.
—JAYME AND LAURA

Contents

Section One

The Adventure of Mentoring

1

Invitation to a Journey

Twenty years from now you will be more disappointed by the things you didn't do than by the ones you did do. So throw off the bowlines, sail away from the safe harbor. Catch the trade winds in your sails. Explore. Dream. Discover.

WIDELY ATTRIBUTED TO MARK TWAIN

What on earth have I gotten myself into?"

A jumbled mess of nerves and excitement, I plopped down on the worn mattress for a breather. My courage faltered as I noticed the sorry version of myself in the mirror. My NYU T-shirt stained with sweat. My hair a hot mess. Surrounded by a sea of yet-to-be-unpacked boxes, bags, and suitcases.

Just hours before, Dad had dropped me off in New York City to officially begin my life as an adult. Unfortunately, he had to stay in our red Ford Pinto so it wouldn't be towed, which meant more trips to unload than I could count.

Up. Down. Up. Down. Lugging all the stuff I had *thought* was essential for this new chapter of life. It's amazing how quickly that perspective changes traversing five flights of stairs!

Amid the noise and traffic and crowds, Dad slipped a piece of money into my hand. "For emergencies," he said with a smile.

Then, with a hug and a kiss and misty eyes, he started the engine, maneuvering our little Pinto out into the flow of taxis and buses.

And just like that, he was gone.

I didn't know whether to laugh or cry. I'd done it! I'd left my tiny Pennsylvania town, Littlestown (no, I'm not joking!), to pursue my dream of becoming a Broadway star. If I squeezed my eyes tightly enough, I could see it—my name in the Playbill as member of the cast in *Annie* or *The King and I*.

Sirens screeched below my window, bringing me back to reality of life as a *grown-up*. Earlier that day, I'd been riding along with Dad, singing Barbra Streisand songs at the top of my lungs. As we drove through the Holland Tunnel, my heart was about to beat out of my chest with anticipation.

Now it was just me . . . in my tiny closet of a room. The city was abuzz with life just below my window, and I was part of it. I was right in the middle of it.

Have you ever found yourself surrounded by people . . . but completely alone?

My roommate, whom I hadn't met yet, wouldn't be arriving for a whole week. As I stared out at the busy street below, I began to have second thoughts. Having grown up in a town of barely three thousand, New York's teeming metropolis of nearly 8 million was just a bit of a culture shock.

How do I make friends in a huge city like this?

How will I ever fall asleep with the sirens and honking and construction drills?

Is it safe to talk to anyone on the street . . . am I safe?

Anxiety turned to fear, and fear grew to sheer panic. I think I was half convinced my own personal bogeyman would break down the door at any moment. I fumbled to find that little folded treasure in my jeans pocket. To my amazement, it was a $100 bill.

"For emergencies," his words echoed in my head.

Well for sure, this is an emergency, I told myself.

Walking all the way up 5th Avenue to 42nd Street—forty-five blocks—I found the Amtrak station as the sun was setting. With a one-way ticket in hand, I boarded the train just in time.

Home. The trip was four hours, giving me plenty of time to practice my spiel. Within less than twenty-four hours of leaving, I was standing once again in our kitchen.

"I made a mistake. I can't do this. Me . . . a Broadway star? It's just a crazy dream."

"Oh, honey, c'mere." Mom put her arms around me and held me tight.

After four days of tearful conversations, pep talks, and prayers, I boarded yet another train. Only this time, I had not one, not two . . . but three folded squares of bills. One from Mom, one from Dad, and one from my sweet grandma.

I don't think they each realized the others also gave me cash, but hey, it worked out fine on my end! And far more than the money, I left with my "love cup" filled up.

You can do this. We believe in you. Their words echoed in my mind as I pressed my face against the glass, the skyline of the city looming ahead.

THE COURAGE TO CONNECT

My roommate Karen and I hit it off surprisingly well, even though I was a night owl, and she was in bed before nine o'clock. After a few minor spats over the light switch, she invested in a sleeping mask, and all was well.

Karen was Jewish, and I was a Christian—or at least a churchgoer. Having grown up with an "us versus them" mentality (*us*, of course, being Christians, and *them* being everyone else), I began to realize as I hung out with Karen how narrow-minded and naïve I'd been. Karen was intelligent, easygoing, funny, and a good listener.

Though we held to differing faiths, we connected over roomie talks that often ended in silliness and raucous laughter. Just being together was fun. We discovered a sublime hole-in-the-wall pizza shop right around the corner and quickly decided that it was *way* better to split a pizza than eat alone . . . even if that did mean eating ridiculously early dinners for her sake.

With the horror stories I'd heard about roommates, I was very thankful to discover a true friend!

The city was still new and overwhelming, but I found myself a little bit less anxious with each passing day. I had found my niche. I fell in love with theatre and music all over again. And yet, something was "off." No matter how many parties I went to, pizzas I consumed, or plays I auditioned for, I could never escape a deep sense of loneliness. Like a black hole that sucked everything away, leaving me completely, utterly alone.

It's hard to exactly put into words, but I wonder if you've felt it, too—an ache for more that you just can't seem to shake.

Our twenties and thirties are an especial time—not the only

time, of course, but a unique time—of pursuing our questions and facing our fears head-on, rather than burying and avoiding them. And so I did.

I rubbed the sleep out of my eyes one Sunday morning, following a late-night concert, and decided to go exploring. To my surprise and delight, I soon found myself in an old opera house–turned sanctuary. I felt like Alice who'd just fallen down the rabbit hole into Wonderland.

Huge chandeliers hung from an expansive gold-plated ceiling.

Heavy velour drapes framed the stage.

The plush theatre-style chairs seemed to go on endlessly.

The opening hymn brought me back from my reverie, and the tune was a familiar one. It seemed rather strange and wonderful all at the same time, singing church songs in a theatre.

I was no stranger to religion. I practically grew up in a church pew. But I always had a lot of questions. *Where does God live? Does Jesus sing? Is He a tenor or a bass?* Mom and Dad were wonderful parents and great role models, but they didn't talk much about faith. They mainly told me about the Golden Rule and the importance of being a "good" girl. I'd tried so hard to be a Goody Two-shoes, but somehow still always managed to track in mud.

After the service was over, I made my way through the crowd to talk with Pastor Paul. My heart was pounding hard.

"I'm new in town. Honestly, I have no clue where to start—with God, with life, with anything, really. I need help. I can't do this alone."

It all tumbled out haphazardly from a place deep inside me . . . a place I wasn't even fully aware of. Seconds later, my brain caught up, and a part of me wished I could stuff that string of words right back in.

You're not a kid anymore, Jayme, my inner critic sneered. *Gosh, play it cool, will you? This is awkward. Stop now before you make it worse.*

But in that moment, I hoped beyond all hope to find a friend. Someone who had walked in my shoes, who wouldn't be scared off by my messiness and questions. Someone who could help me figure out this thing called being a *grown-up*.

DREAMS AND DECISIONS

Perhaps you can relate. You're an adult, technically. You pay bills. You live on your own. You may even have a diploma hanging on your wall. And not a month goes by that you don't give a cut of your paycheck to repay student loans.

But life is . . . well . . . way more complicated than you ever thought.

Alone in a brand-new city, trying to make it in the real world. Your Facebook statuses highlight adventure and excitement, but on the inside, you're feeling a bit unsure of yourself, trying to network, launch your career, make friends, or get a date.

Maybe you've hit the glass ceiling at work and find yourself overworked and underappreciated, just because you're a woman.

Maybe you're stuck in a dead-end job or relationship, and sometimes catch yourself daydreaming of something more. What . . . you're not sure.

Maybe you're newly married, and marriage so far has been the furthest thing from happily ever after.

Or maybe you just broke up with the man you gave your

heart to, and now you wonder if you can ever love again.

A recent study by Barna Group found that nearly 75 percent of women are not sure that they are making the right decisions in life.[1] If that's you, it's most certainly not a mistake that you're reading these words at this moment and place and time. Whether you're sitting in a coffee shop or on the subway, plopped down on your bed at 2:00 a.m., or soaking up the afternoon sunshine at the beach, I believe this book holds a life-changing key to your journey forward.

What are your twenties and thirties for? Having fun? Establishing your career? Seeing the world? Finding the love of your life? Sure, these are all good pursuits. But I would argue that they are each secondary.

I believe that the single most important influence in your life during these years is not what degree you pursue, what job you take, or who you date . . . but who is pouring into your life and shaping you.

A mentor. Perhaps you've heard the term before in business or academic settings, but the Christian community is often behind the curve here. While we tend to emphasize young professionals' groups and women's Bible studies, mentoring is an entirely different experience.

A mentor is a woman, further along in her walk with God than you are, who sees your potential and walks with you in becoming the woman God created you to be.

Just to clarify, she's not your mom and she's not your therapist. She's not someone you pay to spend time with you.

A mentor is a friend, a guide, and a confidante who offers a listening ear, honest feedback, and spiritual encouragement as you navigate each of the secondary pursuits we mentioned above.

She helps you identify and maximize your strengths and giftedness, uncover your calling and passions, and flesh out the day-to-day reality of following Jesus.

This intentional, life-giving, face-to-face relationship holds profound influence in developing you as a woman of God.

Mentoring is like Miracle-Gro for your life—spiritually, emotionally, and relationally.

BECOMING YOUR BEST *YOU*

Sure, it sounds good, Jayme, you may be thinking. *But who would want to mentor ordinary me?* You may come up with a million reasons why it's not feasible, why you don't have time, or why no one would want to invest in you.

But I beg to differ.

Over the last twenty-five years, I've seen time and again how mentoring has the power to change and shape women like you more than any other single thing in the world. Seriously.

I'm not sure about this mentoring thing, you may protest. *I'm kind of supposed to have life figured out by this point, right?* Says who? Is it immature to say you need a mentor? Actually, it's the most mature decision you can make, because growth always happens best in relationship. The Bible references "one another" over a hundred times—from "love one another" to "build one another up" to "pray for one another."

Mentoring is, at its essence, just doing what Jesus said.

I believe all this because I've lived it. From my very first mentor (who you'll hear more about in the next chapter) to the countless women I've had the privilege of walking alongside over the years, mentoring is my heartbeat.

Each week, I have the amazing privilege of meeting one-on-one with women in their twenties and thirties. Some are business executives, others designers, musicians, and artists. They are teachers, doctors, lawyers, counselors . . . they are on the front lines of shaping culture. They are dating, married, divorced, widowed. Some have cute little apartments, others rambunctious little children.

As we sit and talk over lattes or hot chocolate or sweet tea, I am encouraged and inspired by their courage. Their gut-wrenching honesty. Their eagerness to grow and change and become. Their heart to love people and join God in doing good.

Throughout these pages, you'll meet many of these women and get a front-row seat—an uncut version—as they wrestle with self-doubt and fear, explore their passions, identify their calling, and step into their God-given potential.

My greatest fear is that you would spend your twenties and thirties lonely and striving, trying to find your own way . . . just as I did when I first moved to New York City. You may wear yourself out *doing*, while neglecting to focus on the woman you are *becoming*.

And my greatest prayer is that you'll discover the life-giving potential of mentoring for yourself and feel the speed of your personal growth take off.

I promise I'm not being dramatic when I say this single connection has the potential to shape the trajectory of your life more than any other factor I know of.

In the coming chapters, we'll flesh out the practicalities of when, where, how . . . and more. But for now, be encouraged that it's not only possible to connect with a mentor, it's critical in order to become your best *you*.

That's why I sat down with my friend Laura, a twentysomething herself, to write the book you hold in your hands. Really, it's not so much another book as it is an invitation to a journey.

A journey to become the woman God created you to be. And you don't have to walk it alone.

Respond

1. Can you identify with Jayme's transition of leaving family and friends behind and moving to NYC on her own? When have you found yourself in a new and unfamiliar environment?

2. "No matter how many parties I went to, pizzas I consumed, or plays I auditioned for, I could never escape a deep sense of loneliness." Ever been there? What helped you during this time?

3. "The single most important influence in your life during these years is not what degree you pursue, what job you take, or who you date . . . but who is pouring into your life and shaping you." What's your reaction to this perspective? Agree? Disagree? Skeptical? Why?

4. How do you feel about asking for help and admitting that you can't do life alone? Many of us have a hard time with reaching out for support. If that includes you, what holds you back?

5. Nearly 75 percent of women are not sure that they are making the right decisions in life. What areas of your

life do you find yourself worrying and unsure about? Where do you need wisdom right now? What is your hope and desire for the journey of this book?

2

The Influence of a Mentor

When I stand before God at the end of my life, I would hope that I would not have a single bit of talent left, and could say, "I used everything you gave me."

ERMA BOMBECK

'd love to connect you with Jeannie." Pastor Paul's words were so . . . real. No fake ministerial smile or fancy words, just a genuine caring presence.

A flicker of hope in the wasteland of my heart. In this big and bustling city, surrounded by stars and high fashion, I often felt about two inches tall.

Unseen by some. Judged by others. Pegged as "that country girl." Sure, I had friends, but I longed for more.

Maybe, just maybe, I could find someone I could trust. A woman who had been in my shoes. Who would listen and understand and offer wise advice.

Ah, Jeannie. Her warm eyes and inviting smile put me at ease the first time we met.

As we sipped tea, Jeannie's head tilted to the side just a tad, a stray curl falling across her forehead, despite her best attempts to keep it tucked behind her ear. Her face lit up as I talked a mile a minute.

"I feel so incompetent . . . I'm *way* outside my league here." It all came spilling out. "Some days, I just want to stay in bed, pull the covers over my head, and drown out the noise of traffic with *I Love Lucy* reruns."

Surprisingly, Jeannie wasn't put off by my ramblings about my sometimes-crazy acting classes and how hard I was trying to break in to the Broadway scene. She nodded knowingly as I confessed how utterly lonely I felt and how distant God seemed.

The "doer" in me was nearly desperate for a formula to fix it all.

Laughter welled up from deep within Jeannie—a big, hearty laugh—which was okay by me, since my dramatic self wasn't exactly prim and proper either.

"Oh Jayme, just relax! Breathe. It's a journey . . . a journey we're on. Not a flowchart! You and me both. I still don't have it all figured out."

"But," she continued with a twinkle in her eye, "we're not alone."

Jeannie went on to share her own struggles with finding faith, how lost she felt when she first moved to the city, and the ways God had shown up unexpectedly when she was facing career decisions.

It was new . . . different. Some of the women in my church

growing up were sweet and loving, but seemed more concerned with who was bringing what dish to the potluck than they were about sharing real gut-honest tough stuff.

In fact, I'd learned early on in life that makeup and a happy "Christian" smile go hand in hand; you put both on in the morning before you walk out the door.

But what about the ache I felt? Did that not matter at all?

Jeannie said that yes, it did matter. She encouraged me that the angst . . . the questions . . . the longing for something deeper . . . wasn't just me going through a funk. It was God Himself, awakening my heart to know Him more. Not just as an abstract idea, but as a real living presence in my riding-the-subway, practicing-my-lines daily life.

Little did I know that day we shared our first cup of tea how great an influence Jeannie would become in my life. Her life-giving relationship would equip me with wisdom and discernment to navigate *a lot* of tough decisions.

LEARNING TO LISTEN, LEARNING TO PRAY

Jeannie met me on Thursday afternoons at Zabar's, a café tucked away on the upper west side. Over coffee and cappuccinos and New York bagels slathered with cream cheese, we talked about life. Auditions. Roommates. Missing home. My boyfriend. Career decisions. How to live on *nothing*. And God.

I always thought God was for church . . . for Sundays . . . but as we went along, I began to realize He was right at the center of it all. My messiness. My dreams. My fears.

Over the next few months, Jeannie taught me to pray conversationally. To talk to God just like I would a friend. To honestly share my heart, holding nothing back . . . then soak in the stillness and listen for His voice.

To not view prayer as a spiritual activity but a continual conversation. It was strange, at first—it felt so vulnerable. I was used to reading prayers out of a book.

What if I don't say the right thing?

But as Jeannie and I began to read Scripture together, I was amazed to see how some of those folks talked to God.

David got pretty angry with God sometimes, and Jonah bluntly told God he'd rather die than live. Hannah begged God for a son—tears and all—and I started to not feel so bad after all. Maybe God can take it.

"Maybe God already knows the deepest darkest secrets of our hearts, and loves us anyway," Jeannie reflected, pointing to 1 John 3:20 (ESV), "God is greater than our heart, and he knows everything."

I was intrigued at how the Bible seemed chock-full of people whose lives were marked by flaws and failures, yet God still did some pretty amazing things through them. Moses killed a man in anger, yet God used him to lead the Israelites out of slavery. David committed adultery with Bathsheba, but God still called him "a man after my own heart."

And Peter—Peter was my favorite. The guy walked on water in the middle of a storm. He passed out bread and fish to five thousand plus people, all from one kid's lunch, but in a moment of fear denied even knowing Jesus.

Could God have a plan for me too? As I dove more deeply into Scripture and peppered Jeannie with questions week after week, the answer became a resounding yes. Like John, I wanted to walk with Jesus and hang on to His every word. Like Mary, I wanted to sit at His feet. Like Peter, I wanted to boldly declare His truth to anyone who would listen.

God had always seemed distant and aloof, but I began to see in real time how He was pursuing me and guiding my every step. My roommate Karen's dad just *happened* to be a mainstream producer in the city. Talk about providence! I was floored when, during my junior year at NYU, he offered me a recording contract. I squealed like a little girl! I was breaking in to the performance world, on a career track with my sights on Broadway.

The next six months were a blur of vocal lessons, practicing rooms, rehearsal studios, meetings with producers, and late nights . . . every night. I was exhausted. My body was worn down from lack of sleep and nutrition, and way too much caffeine.

More often than not, my daily sustenance consisted of pizza, hot dogs, or similar fare that I grabbed at a street stand and ate on the run, followed by late-night bingeing on sweets to keep my energy up. Buying groceries was a luxury I didn't have time for.

Everything was finally falling into place, but I had no peace. I felt frazzled, stressed, and overcommitted. I couldn't sleep at night, and lay in bed exhausted and worrying.

SEARCHING FOR ANSWERS

"What's happening to me?" I begged Jeannie for answers. But rather than telling me what to do, she directed me where to go.

Jeannie taught me about discernment, decision-making, and finding God's direction. Looking to Scripture, I started putting my name in all the blanks where Jesus was talking:

"Come, follow me, Jayme . . ." (Matthew 4:19)

"[You] shall not live by bread alone, Jayme, but by every word that comes from the mouth of God" (Matthew 4:4 ESV).

"Do not be anxious about anything, Jayme, but in everything by prayer and supplication with thanksgiving let your requests be made known to God" (Philippians 4:6 ESV).

"Without faith it is impossible to please God, Jayme . . . believe that he exists and that he rewards those who earnestly seek him" (Hebrews 11:6).

I begged God for clarity. And while I didn't see handwriting on the wall, after a lot of tears, cancelled rehearsals, and conversations with Jeannie, my fiancé, and my family, I knew.

Turn down the contract . . . and trust Me, I sensed God saying. *Trust Me that I have something even better in store for you just ahead.*

It seemed so counterintuitive.

A high-profile recording deal was a no-brainer, right? After all, this was why I'd moved to the city—to build my career. And with a bigger platform and more visibility, I told myself, I'd have countless opportunities to make a positive Christian impact in the entertainment industry.

Faith. It had always been a nice-sounding theological word to me. Nothing more. But living it? Giving up control? Absolutely terrifying!

My producer had paved my path to success, but as hard as I tried to make it work in my brain, it just didn't. I was sacrificing my health, my sanity, and even my relationship with my fiancé in the pursuit of one thing.

My life was way out of balance, and I was about to crash and burn. I was so vulnerable to getting sucked in to the glamour and glitz of the spotlight. I can see now how God protected me from selling out to my career at the expense of every other aspect of my being.

Turning down the recording contract was the first big decision I ever made for myself. The weight of responsibility was sobering—no one could tell me exactly what to do. I had to seek God for myself, listen to His voice, get godly advice . . . and eventually, step out in faith and cut myself loose. It hurt—God seemed to be asking me to walk away from my dreams. I was scared and conflicted, yet I knew God had a plan for my good, even if I couldn't fully see it yet.

Honestly, I don't think I could have made it through this season without Jeannie. It's difficult to tease out God's direction, especially when there seems to be multiple good options. Jeannie walked with me through every step—helping me weigh the pros and cons, praying with me, and seeing the potential I couldn't see in myself.

The potential to be an influencer, not just a glamour girl.

I share all this with you as a real-life picture of just how powerful a mentoring relationship can be in your life trajectory. Mentoring is not a formula or a checklist; it's a relationship. The arrangements of time and place will vary—and that's the beauty of it. It may look like having lunch together, grabbing coffee after work, or chatting while your little ones are napping. You can make mentoring work for you, no matter what your schedule or pace of life.

Far from asking me to give up my career, God was at work to help me discover the specific areas where He wanted me to invest my time and energy. I don't know if I could've had a career on Broadway, or if anyone would've bought the album that I was going to record. But looking back all these years later, what I do know is that I have no regrets.

I went to Broadway to become a star, but the stage lights quickly grew dim as I realized that God was inviting me into a much bigger story—an eternal story. He was the screenwriter and producer, and He had written a part just for me.

I thought I'd been cast as a main stage actress, with a solo ballad and multiple dramatic scenes. But God's storyline for me developed instead through speaking, writing, and pouring into women's lives through mentoring. Every week, I now have the privilege of walking with women through the messiness of life, and helping them discover who God created them to be.

Just as Jeannie walked with me.

MENTORING IN REAL LIFE

Naomi mentored Ruth. Jesus mentored His disciples. Paul mentored Timothy. Elizabeth mentored Mary . . . and the list goes on. In Scripture, in literature, and throughout history, mentoring has played a critical role in personal and spiritual development.

And I am convinced it's the missing link in the church today. I believe mentoring isn't just a nice idea. It's critical for your growth—professionally, emotionally, relationally, and spiritually. Mentoring can make the difference between success and significance. Between performing at work and developing your potential. Between doing and becoming.

Perhaps the most often-quoted (and at times cliché) "mentoring" passage in Christian circles is Titus 2:3–5 (NLT). Let's take a fresh look:

Teach the older women to live in a way that honors God. They must not slander others or be heavy drinkers. Instead, they should teach others what is good. These older women must train the younger women to love their husbands and their children, to live wisely and be pure, to work in their homes, to do good, and to be submissive to their husbands.

In biblical culture, women often married and had children at a young age. You may find yourself pursuing your education or a career or chasing little ones around the house. The point here isn't so much *what you do* as it is *how you live.* What does it look like to live in a way that honors God? A mentor can help you discover that. According to Scripture, a mentor should be a mature Christian woman willing and able to serve by giving another woman biblical counsel to equip her to *do life God's way.* Some relationships are long-term, while other mentors may only be in your life for a season, but regardless, meeting one-on-one with another woman will habitually produce the most growth in every area of your life.

Notice that nowhere in Titus 2 does Paul say the word "perfect." Perfect Christian mentors do not exist and never will. We're human! As long as we're in these earthly bodies, wrestling daily with our sinful natures, we each need God's grace and forgiveness. Often, that's the lightbulb moment that happens as we sit with a mentor.

You doubt God too sometimes and struggle to hold on to faith?

You have a hard time saying no at work and often overfill your plate?

You face disappointment and have to grieve dreams that haven't come true?

You lose your temper and say things you regret?

By reaching out for help and support, we can experience solidarity with other women on the journey. We realize we are not the only one struggling, and we can focus our energy on growing in godly character together, rather than hiding or pretending we have it all together.

This is the key we've been missing: growth doesn't happen well in isolation. We can never become all God intends for us to be only through quiet times and Bible studies.

Some things in life we can only know through experience, because growth always happens in relationship—in connection—in community.

Over the past thirty-five years since I first met Jeannie, God has blessed me with many mentors who have poured into my life and helped me flesh out the day-to-day realities of following Christ. I can't imagine going through my young married years, my kids' terrible twos, career transitions, the deaths of my parents . . . and countless other rattling life events alone without mentors being there for me in my darkest moments.

The heartbeat of this book is to connect you with God and with other women. Women you can trust with the deepest parts of your story. Women who will walk with you through the fog of confusion and the mire of disappointment. Women who will be there to celebrate God's goodness and provision in your life. Women who will challenge you to dig deep . . . and unearth the calling and passions God has placed inside you.

It may sound counterintuitive, but connecting with a mentor actually starts with knowing yourself (so don't pick up your phone just yet!). In order to identify the areas we each need to grow in, we must slow down to face our fears and insecurities and listen to God.

"We are a 'doing' people," Henry Blackaby writes. "We always want to be doing something."[1] *Work harder. Take on more. Make a difference.*

But it will ultimately leave us empty and disillusioned. In contrast, "God is crying out and shouting to us, 'Don't just do something. Stand there!'"[2]

Stop. Wait. Listen.

"Enter into a love relationship with Me," God invites us. "Get to know Me. Adjust your life to Me. Let Me love you and reveal Myself to you as I work through you."[3]

Many of us can be very eager to do something *for* God. Sure, we can do some good things in our own strength, but apart from God, none of it will have an eternal impact.

It's the difference between a good thing and a God thing. As we slow down and tune in to His heart, we'll come to understand the way God is working around us, and our role in that. We'll unearth the potential God has placed deep inside us, and the role He has for us to play in His story of healing and redemption.

"Don't be in a hurry . . . Don't try to skip over the relationship to get on with the activity."[4] Certainly, our relationship with Him comes first, but also important is our relationship with other women.

So as we wrap up this chapter, I encourage you to take a moment to quiet your heart. Ask God to give you insight into the areas you need to grow in, then jot down whatever He brings to your mind.

Let's purpose together that when we stand before God one

day, we'll be able to joyously say, "I used everything You gave me." No unused talent. No hidden fears. No regrets . . . because, in community with other Christian women, we relentlessly pursued growth.

Respond

1. Have you experienced prayer as a conversation before? Take a fresh look at 1 John 3:20. When you reflect on God being at the center of your dreams, fears, and messiness, how does that change the way you approach Him?

2. What things in your life would you label "good things" versus "God things"? Have you ever faced a tough decision to turn down a good opportunity? How did you handle it?

3. Jayme writes, "I thought I'd been cast as a main stage actress." Where do you see your part in God's storyline currently? What crossroads are you facing in your life? How can you seek God in the middle of it?

4. What comes to mind when you hear the word "mentoring"? Reflect on your experiences with mentoring, both positive and negative. Do you have any mentoring baggage to work through?

5. In what areas in your life are you focused mostly on doing and need to grow into becoming? How can you begin incorporating rhythms of waiting, listening, and seeking God before jumping to act?

3

Messy Faith

> *Her life isn't perfect—sometimes it's messy.
> But what makes her different from any other
> girl is her relationship with the Creator of
> the universe. She isn't just interested in God.
> She's connected with him.*
> HAYLEY DIMARCO

Something's missing . . . and I'm not sure what. The light shows, the trendy sermons, the Sunday morning performance. I'm searching for Jesus, crying out to hear Him . . . to find Him somehow in the midst of it.

"I need wisdom, Jayme. I need answers. But all I hear is noise. Noise that echoes my own inner chaos."

The women I mentor continually challenge me. Their authenticity pushes me toward deeper honesty with God and with myself. On this particular day, frustration was written all over my friend's face.

"Gosh, life is a lot more complicated than what they told me in Sunday school as a kid," she said with a smile. "Honestly,

I don't have a clue what I'm doing, and a lot of my ideas about God are getting blown up. Sometimes I worry about what will be left!

"I feel like my faith is unraveling at the seams. Growing up, I believed in Christianity because, as church folk say, 'The Bible says it, I believe it, and that settles it.' Now, everything seems fuzzy and unclear, and I just don't know.

"I sit in church, but rather than taking notes on the sermon, I'm picking it apart. Writing down questions. Googling the pastor's examples to see if they're even correct.

"It seems like the church is little more than a social club, all of us showing off the outfit we chose and looking spiritual. Why do so many people spend a lifetime playing games, but ignoring issues that really matter?

"It's so fake. To be honest, I feel more welcomed and accepted by my coworkers at happy hour than by church people.

"It's easy to point the finger, but recently, I've been realizing . . . it's me, too. I'm going through the motions, but there's no life in it. I'm drifting, and God seems so distant. Sometimes I wonder if He even cares. Because I see Him show up for other people, but not for me.

"What does it actually look like to follow Jesus—for real? To know Him like the disciples did. For the truth of who He is to actually change the way I live . . ."

I admired her courage to ask hard questions, rather than sugarcoating reality. To bring her doubts and fears to the table, holding nothing back. She could have answered my question "How are you and God doing?" quite differently. She could have said, "Pretty good . . . I've just been busy."

But in that moment, her desire to grow won out over her

need to be put together. My friend took the plunge of honesty. She dared to believe that somehow in the midst of our long talks, God would show up.

THE ACHE FOR MORE

Have you felt it? That ache for a safe place to "dump your truck," as I like to say. To let it all out. To be completely you—the questioning, overwhelmed, insecure you behind your confident persona—and be loved for who you are. To feel safe to talk about your darkest secrets and scariest questions. To wrestle through doubts you have about God and know that you'll get honest and biblical input, not just feel-good answers.

The modern-day idea of church is a bit ironic. We're all focused on one person—it's a monologue. No dialogue. No discussion. No connection.

We put on our nice clothes, jockey for a great parking spot, and listen as the pastor shares a message about living the Christian life. Maybe we even have a religious experience and feel "close" to God.

For an hour once a week. But I wonder, is this what God intended for the body of Christ? Think about the other 167 hours in your week. The night before His crucifixion, Jesus prayed for us, and the cry of His heart was, "Father, give them amazing programs, deep, intellectual sermons, and Sunday morning productions that rock the building."

Far from it! He begged God, "that all of them may be one, Father, just as you are in me and I am in you" (John 17:21). God created us for face-to-face relationships, and we can't thrive without them, no matter how vast our social media platform is!

When God said, "It is not good for man to be alone" (Genesis 2:18), He wasn't just referencing marriage. He was speaking to the deep human need for connection—single and married—to be known at the deepest parts of who we are, behind the makeup, the online status, and the plastic smile.

Well before the command to "do"—to take dominion over the earth through pursuing our calling and building our career—God placed primary importance on relationship. But the American dream doesn't always do that. It's so easy to squelch that longing. To tell ourselves, "You're an adult. Figure it out on your own. And whatever you do, don't make a fool of yourself!"

And so we pull back. We draw inside ourselves, and often, insecurity and shame wreak havoc. We build walls and decorate them with our accomplishments. And tragically, we tune out that reckless voice that says, "I need help. I can't do this alone."

Herein lies the dilemma: Hide-and-seek isn't just a childhood game. I learned from other women growing up how to hide my messiness behind a carefully crafted mask. Masks come in all different shapes and sizes. Theatrical masks to perform and get attention. Cucumber facial masks to get rid of blemishes. Or maybe even a baseball catcher's mask to protect from messiness not of our own choosing.

We can put on a *strong* mask saying, "I've got this on my own." Or the *smile* mask of "I'm always doing great!" Or the infamous *church* mask, because after all, once you make a commitment to follow Jesus, your life is supposed to be redeemed, restored, and pretty much perfect, right?

Every morning, I would put on my mask with my makeup. I tried to convince everyone around me that I had life all figured out. When I did take the risk to be honest, the end result was rarely positive. People around me were often too busy to truly engage at a heart level. And when I shared my fears or hurts, it wasn't long before I heard it repeated as the latest "prayer request" that spread like wildfire.

Our negative experiences with other women often only reinforce our habit of doing life alone. But what if the rugged individualism that we so often wear as a badge of honor is actually sabotaging the process of our growth?

Could it be that the key to discovering who we truly are lies not in working longer hours or putting more energy into networking . . . but *in relationship* with God and other women?

REDEFINING "GROWN-UP"

Being grown-up equals being put together, or at least that's what I learned. From perfect makeup and every hair in place to a poised presence and just the right response in a conversation . . . it's a lot to keep up with!

But what if just the opposite were true? What if maturing and truly growing up means owning and addressing our weaknesses. Being comfortable and confident in our own skin. Leaning into growth and seeking it out rather than pretending we don't need to grow!

Consider God's creation. Grass grows. Trees produce new foliage each spring. And each day in our own bodies, nearly two trillion new cells are created. If any living thing is not producing new growth, it is slowly dying. And we are no exception! Following Jesus is not so much about making a decision or praying a prayer as it is about embracing a lifelong process of growing, changing, and being transformed to the image of Christ (see 2 Corinthians 3:18).

I've come to realize over the years that if your life isn't messy, you are probably messed up. It's so easy to live in denial and convince both ourselves and others that we are fine. But the reality is that we actually become our healthiest when we admit we have a messy life, because only then are we getting to the true issues God wants to address and transform.

Consider the scene of any creative work. A painter's canvas. A kitchen on Christmas Eve. A house under construction. A sculpture in process. All of these scenarios have one thing in common—messiness. "Clutter and mess show us that life is being lived," author Anne Lamott writes. "Certainty is missing the point entirely. Faith includes noticing the mess, the emptiness and discomfort, and letting it be there until some light returns."[1]

Faith is not just believing abstract ideas about God, it's having the courage to walk that out in our lives. This necessitates that we unravel false doctrines, let go of legalism, and bury the man-made religion by which we may have defined ourselves. It's realizing that our personal views are not inerrant, and that the rules we've clung so tightly to in order to define ourselves may actually be idols.

This journey of rediscovering the true gospel is one of raw honesty, and often, deep pain. It will change you, but it is not an easy road to travel.

It's a huge relief to realize that *messy* is what a healthy relationship with Jesus looks like. That's genuine faith. God never created you to be perfect or to do your relationship with Him solo. Hiding and pretending only hampers your growth.

When we stop pretending and hiding, we can actually invest our energy in changing and growing. And that's the best place of all to live! Where you are right now is where you are—and we are all imperfect. So don't minimize it or hide your weaknesses and failures. Instead, own them. Bring them into the light. Because that's exactly the space God longs to transform.

Fighting to live in this space day by day isn't easy, though. We're swimming upstream in a culture that is all about image and performance. It takes a lot of humility to be honest about where we're at and what we need.

But this is a critical step in the journey of mentoring. God created us as women to learn from and support one another. To stick together in life's darkest moments. No matter how hard we try, we can't flourish in isolation (or behind our computer screens!).

Knowing we need safe friendships isn't enough, because research suggests that these sorts of relationships are few and far between. Nearly one in three women in their twenties and one in five women in their thirties relocate to a different city or state each year . . . often away from the support of extended family and longtime friends.[2] More than half of the women surveyed in one study felt they didn't have a strong support system, and over one in three admitted that they often feel lonely.[3]

Across the board—for professionals who are building their careers, stay-at-home moms with young kids, and women who are faced with divorce or widowhood—lack of relational support is rampant.

"We live in the most connected yet disconnected age since the Garden of Eden," author Brandon Cox reflects. "We are split seconds away from communicating with anyone on the planet, and there are more ways to meet more new people than ever before, but we are lonelier than ever."[4]

Being a woman in today's world is hard enough, as most of us juggle multiple roles. But going through life with the deep inner presumption that "I am alone in this" can push any of us to the breaking point. Add in the social pressure and not-so-subtle messaging that we are important in the eyes of the world when we are overcommitted, rushed, and crazy busy, and the result is *anything but* living out our full potential.

Honesty with yourself and with safe people is key. Connecting authentically requires risk, and maybe that's why it's so easy to hold on to our masks. We might get hurt. We might feel misunderstood. We might be rejected. That's why honesty must go hand in hand with wisdom in the relationships we seek to cultivate. I'm not talking about over sharing, pouring your heart out to every person you meet. That can actually be quite destructive.

But how do you know if someone is safe? What makes a woman a good potential mentor? In a new city or a new job, it's easy to feel surrounded by people but all alone. That's why we're journeying through these pages together . . . step by step . . . to prepare and equip you with discernment as you begin to seek out a mentor.

LIVE YOUR QUESTIONS

We all long for certainty. It's innate to our human nature. But for many of us, our twenties and thirties are about anything *but* certainty! That's why finding a mentor you can trust will keep you grounded and give you courage to live your questions. As writer Rainer Maria Rilke admonishes,

Have patience with everything that is unsolved in your heart and try to cherish the questions themselves, like closed rooms and like books written in a very strange tongue. Do not search now for the answers which cannot be given you because you could not live them. It is a matter of living everything. Live the questions now. Perhaps you will then gradually, without noticing it, one distant day live right into the answer.[5]

Rilke aptly describes a critical element of mentoring: bringing our questions, doubts, fears, and dreams into the light of a safe relationship. I learned early on in being mentored by Jeannie that there are often more questions than answers in life, particularly during seasons of transition and change.

What does it look like to love like Jesus when our boss discredits our work, when our best friend betrays us, when the kids are screaming?

How do we make sense of life when our car gets totaled, when the cancer screen comes back positive, when we feel the crushing weight of aloneness?

How do we weigh multiple good options—job offers, ministry opportunities, and relationships—and know where to invest our time and energy?

Where is God . . . and why hasn't He shown up to protect and provide for us as the Bible promises?

When we can't feel God, when questions and doubts cloud the vision of our faith, we must stop and ask ourselves, *Have I been following the church, following my small group leader, or following Jesus?*

Along the way, we may just discover that "doubt is a question mark; faith is an exclamation point" and "the most compelling, believable, realistic stories have included them both."[6] This is one of the reasons I love the biblical story of Thomas. He's just so *real*. So down to earth. So like me. He certainly wasn't afraid to admit his questions! The disciples are all excited and high-fiving each other because they've seen Jesus—alive. But Thomas is pretty skeptical. *Maybe it's just wishful thinking. Maybe they just imagined it. Maybe it was a ghost.*

"I won't believe it unless I see it myself!" he tells his buddies. "Unless I see the nail marks in his hands and put my finger where the nails were, and put my hand into his side . . ." (John 20:25).

Talk about honesty about where he was at! A few days later, as the disciples are gathered together, Jesus walks right through a locked door. And Thomas sees.

"'Peace be with you!'" Jesus greets his friends. "Then he said to Thomas, 'Put your finger here; see my hands. Reach out your hand and put it into my side'" (John 20:26–27).

I love Jesus' warm invitation to Thomas. This is a beautiful picture of the mentoring relationship. Jesus isn't surprised, angry, belittling, or avoidant. Thomas had lots of questions and doubts, but Jesus never said, "Shut up" or "Get over it."

Quite the contrary! Jesus lovingly reaches out to Thomas—and to us—assuring us of the true reality of the situation: *I am alive. I am here . . . with you and for you.*

Thomas takes it all in. The freshly healed scars. The tenderness in Jesus' voice. The piercing love in his Master's eyes. And everything begins to change.

"My Lord and my God!" Thomas gasps. I imagine him running into Jesus' arms, crying on His chest, breathing in new life.

"Because you have seen me, you have believed," Jesus responds. "Blessed are those who have not seen and yet have believed" (John 20:29). Across two millennia, Jesus speaks directly to you. To me.

Faith is a journey, a journey that we dare not take alone. We need courage to ask hard questions. We need wisdom to discern God's leading. While Jesus is always present with us, a safe person—our mentor—can help us connect and find God in the messiness of our questions, doubts, and confusion.

Before you turn the page, why not jot down below some of the biggest questions you're wrestling with? Unless you're first honest with yourself, you'll struggle to be honest with a mentor.

Together, we'll begin to seek out safe people who can walk with you in living those questions day by day. Along the journey, you can rest in knowing that God is the great orchestrator of all good gifts, including, and perhaps especially, the gift of a mentor.

Respond

1. Have you ever felt jaded by the church? If so, why? Write out or share some of your questions and the areas where you're confused and questioning.

2. "Hide-and-seek isn't just a childhood game." What did you learn from the women in your life growing up about performing and pretending? In what ways do you hide?

3. How would you define being grown-up? How does God define it? Jayme shares 2 Corinthians 3:18. Identify

several other Scriptures that talk about growth. What is the common theme here?

4. "No matter how hard we try, we can't flourish in isolation . . . [but] honesty must go hand in hand with wisdom in the relationships we seek to cultivate." What are the fears you have about being honest and vulnerable? How do you know if someone is safe?

5. What would it look like for you to live your questions? How does Jesus' response to Thomas encourage you? In what ways can you embrace your doubts and uncertainties as a key part of your faith journey?

Section Two:

Connecting with a Mentor

4

Living on Purpose: How to Find a Mentor

*Clarity is power: once you're clear about
what you were put here to do then "jobs"
become only a means toward accomplishing
your mission, not an end in themselves.*

LAURIE BETH JONES

I want a purpose that's about more than climbing the career
ladder, buying more stuff, and retiring early. That doesn't
make my heart beat faster at all.

"I want my life to count. I want to really make a difference,
not just make a lot of money. Hey," she said with a laugh. "I'm not
even very good at that!"

My friend had just gotten the news that her department was
being downsized, and she was being laid off. That same day, her
husband had been offered a management position with a company
in Nevada. The decision made sense on paper, but certainly not
emotionally!

"I feel like my world is spinning out of control! What am I going to do? I don't know a single soul in Las Vegas, and I'm unemployed. Plus, it's the desert! I've been trying to remind myself that God is somehow in this. That it's part of His plan for Jake and me. But I worry—a lot!

"What if no one will hire me in Las Vegas? Or I end up in a horrible job?

"How will we meet people and make new friends? How will we find a church?

"What if I can't find another mentor? How do I even begin to say goodbye to my friends here in Atlanta—and to you!?"

Tears welled up in both our eyes. Over the past three years, we'd shared countless cups of coffee, long walks, and lunches. We'd talked about God, relationships, and living out her purpose. Not just career or educational goals, but discovering the passions God had put in her heart.

It would be a hard goodbye. But I was so proud of her, stepping authentically into this next season. She was honest. Reflective. Seeking wisdom. And that is beautiful soil for growth.

"I'm twenty-seven . . . and I'm back at square one." She sighed. "New state, new coworkers, new neighborhood, new friends, new small group, new hairstylist . . . and I guess, a new me, too!

"It's pretty overwhelming. Nobody gets a degree in how to build a life. Find community. Start over in a new place. And especially, connect with a new mentor."

I remember feeling the same way with each of our moves. Questioning. Unsure of myself. Afraid. And I also remember the fruit. A thousand moments and people who changed and shaped and grew me. As those memories came rushing back, I leaned forward excitedly.

"I know it's a bit disorienting right now, and it doesn't all make sense. But I can't wait to see what God is up to in your life right around the corner!"

It would stretch her, leaving behind everything—and everyone—familiar. But she, and you and I, are faced each new day with choices and opportunities that we dare not miss.

Are you drifting along through life, or stepping each day into your God-given purpose?

SETTING SAIL, FIGHTING GIANTS

I love looking out at the colorful sailboats when we visit the beach. Some sails are beautiful hues of blue. Others, red or purple. The first step to setting out on any voyage is hoisting your sails. Otherwise, the wind will blow on by, leaving your boat bobbing in the waves, adrift with the current.

To actually catch the wind in your sails, your boat must be positioned at just the right angle. Try to sail straight into the wind, and you'll hit the "no-go zone"—your sails will flap aimlessly, and you'll lose all momentum. Lose track of your bearings, and you'll run aground.

Sailing takes focused attention. You've got to know your boat, watch the wind, and stay at the helm to readjust the rudder. Life is that way, too. Discovering your purpose and living out your calling requires the same intentionality and action.

Across the seasons of your life, you'll likely find yourself in many different environments. You'll work different jobs. Live in different cities. Make different friends. And learn from different mentors. Each of these experiences is another page in your story, but the binding—what holds all the pages together—is your purpose.

It's what you were created for. It's bigger than just your career, your hobbies, your successes or your failures. You may not see it all right now, but God uses everything. Your mistakes, your pain, your weakness. Your passions, your burdens, your dreams. It's all part of the purpose God is sewing into the binding of your life.

Consider the story of Joshua. Growing up a slave in Egypt, Joshua had little to dream about. Get through the day alive, and fall asleep exhausted. No hint of divine purpose here.

Joshua was just a young man in his twenties when he walked through the Red Sea on dry ground. He felt the ground shake as those same waves came crashing down on the most powerful army in the world. Joshua seemed like just an ordinary fella—one in a million.

But this guy stood out of the crowd. A clear leader, he was chosen for a recon mission into Canaan. Spying out the land God had promised them, the twelve scouts were surprised at what they found: "It does flow with milk and honey! Here is its fruit!" They reported back. "But the people who live there are powerful, and the cities are fortified and large. We even saw descendants of [the giant] Anak there" (Numbers 13:27–29).

Frightened by what they saw, ten of the spies tucked tail and ran. But not Joshua and his buddy Caleb. "The land we passed through and explored is exceedingly good. If the Lord is pleased with us, he will lead us into that land . . . Only do not rebel against the Lord! And do not be afraid of the people of the land, because we will devour them" (Numbers 14:6–9).

Joshua and Caleb believed, but the rest of Israel didn't. Imagine spending your next forty years wandering around in the desert because of someone else's disobedience, saying goodbye to your friends one by one as they died. I would've been angry and bitter!

Instead, Joshua watched and learned from his mentor Moses. When the people were discouraged and complaining, Joshua was all ears. He watched how Moses sought God for wisdom, advocated for the people, resolved conflicts, and led the emerging nation. I wonder when it clicked for Joshua, when he finally got the big picture: *I'm the one who will replace Moses.* Every single step—from slave to spy to wanderer—was a key part in Joshua's calling.

Nothing was wasted. What's your personal wilderness? Pastor Andy Stanley encourages us, "God is using your circumstances to prepare you to accomplish his vision for your life . . . You are not wasting your time. You are not spinning your wheels. If you are 'seeking first' his kingdom where you are . . . he has positioned you there with a purpose in mind."[1]

When Moses died, Joshua was in his sixties—in our timeline, he would have been getting ready to retire. But not in God's plan. In order for Joshua to lead effectively, he needed a deep and intimate relationship with God, where he could hear God's voice and then step out in obedience. Is it any wonder that God called Joshua to those forty years of listening and learning?

Without that time of preparation, Joshua may have dismissed God's leading to march around Jericho as crazy talk and succumbed to the temptation to fight head-on. And that would not have been the result God desired!

DISCOVERING YOUR CALLING

Go after your dreams, seize the moment, be whoever you want to be, the world tells us. But I've got news. Purpose isn't something you create for yourself. You discover it, just like a sailor who unfurls those big, beautiful sails catches the wind on a summer day.

"Many are the plans in a person's heart, but it is the Lord's purpose that prevails" (Proverbs 19:21). Often, our God-given purpose is buried deep under years of expectations. Who we "should be." Who our parents want us to be. Even who we think we want to be. Unearthing our divine purpose requires peeling back fears and insecurities and taking a good look at our career ambitions. In the rat race of life, it's easy to get tunnel vision and think that our purpose equals our career. But that's dreaming way too small. John Ortberg wisely writes:

> A calling, which is something I do for God, is [easily] replaced by a career, which threatens to become my god. A career is something I choose for myself; a calling is something I receive. A career is something I do for myself; a calling is something I do for God.[2]

A mentor can't tell you what your calling is, but she can walk with you in discovering it. Here are some clues to keep in mind, some things you'll want to go over with your mentor.

As God's daughters, we are first of all called into an intimate relationship with Him—to know Him and soak up His love. Are you a daughter of God? If you're not sure, let's go over what that means.

The question is not what do you think of Christ; the question is what have you done about what you think? This is the perfect time to take care of that.

Picture this. All of God's wrath and anger was poured out on Christ at the cross and will not be poured out on you and me if we are in Christ. God gives us the intelligence to think, and then gives us the choice to be courageous and act.

Christ came to forgive us and release us from our prison of guilt. He is waiting for you to give Him control and open your heart to Him. Won't you let Him in and come face-to-face with the reality of Jesus Christ's death and resurrection? Be authentic with God. Don't put this decision off another day. Pray and acknowledge that Jesus has the right to rule in your life and be glorified, as you trust Him alone for eternal life.

Having a personal relationship with Jesus is who I am and how I live. It's not about where I go to church or what I do—it's a heart issue. Jesus bridges the gap between my aloneness and God. First Timothy 2:5 says, "There is one God, and there is one mediator between God and mankind, the man Christ Jesus."

I still mess up and need to ask for forgiveness, but having an authentic relationship with Jesus gives me the grace to move forward. We don't need to do life alone.

The only wind that will propel you forward into a life of purpose is the wind of His Spirit, not the gusts of ambition and striving. Jen Pollock Michel reminds us, "There is never a work we do *for* God apart from a vision *of* God and communion *with* God."[3]

We're also called into relationships with other people—to care and serve and give ourselves away. To harness our gifts, talents, and personality to make a difference and love our neighbor.

It's easy to glamorize this idea of purpose, assuming that God's calling us to something big and visible and world changing, like starting a nonprofit or going on a mission trip. But most often, our calling is found in the mundane of day-to-day living. Loving God *there*. Serving our neighbor *there*. Need does not necessarily equal call, because there are hundreds of ways you could love your neighbor. But you are not called to all of them.

One of your biggest clues to discovering your unique purpose is looking at your desires and passions and aligning them with God's. What do you enjoy doing? What are you good at? What makes you feel alive? God has wired your purpose into your brain and woven it into your heart. "The place God calls you to is the place where your deep gladness and the world's deep hunger meet," Fredrick Buechner points out.[4] Where your passions and burdens intersect with people's needs.

Your purpose isn't about making a name for yourself, it's about joining God in the work He is already doing: "The plans of the Lord stand firm forever, the purposes of his heart through all generations" (Psalm 33:11). God has hand-fashioned you with a unique role to play in the grand story of redemption. Your purpose is not a physical place, either, but a way of being. A way of loving, of living, of walking out Jesus—no matter where you live or what job you work at the moment. It's the unique way you bring beauty and hope and healing to our world.

More often than not, our purpose won't show up as handwriting on a wall. And with each new season, it will likely shift a bit, just like the wind. So rather than just filling in the blank "My life purpose is to _____" and moving on, I encourage you to build a life that is rich in relationships. Joshua had Moses and Caleb . . . who do you have?

COOKOUTS AND COMMUNITY

When John and I first moved to Florida, I was lonelier than I'd ever been in my life. Talk about a shift in my purpose! I'd left behind my Broadway ambitions and was trying to learn how to run a cash register at my multiple part-time jobs. I didn't feel like I was good at *anything*. One evening, while lugging groceries inside, I noticed a sign on the announcement board: Apartment-wide Summer Cookout.

Why not? I figured. It sounded like a great way to meet people. Then began the several-day torment of what outfit I should wear—*is that too dressy? Or too country?* Deciding what to bring as a side wasn't much better, since spaghetti and grilled cheese were my main specialties.

Looking back now, I don't remember what I wore or what dish we brought. But for the first time in months, I felt hope. Hope that I could once again be known. Everyone at the cookout was in a similar spot: new to the area, didn't know anyone, working long hours.

That day I met Joy, who had a degree in interior design and had just graduated from cooking school. Talk about intimidating! I wanted to duck and run. Looking back, I'm so glad I didn't. Joy and I and a few others from the cookout became fast friends.

We never formed a small group or anything official like that. We just got together and cooked every Thursday night. Chicken casserole. Shrimp and veggies. Burgers. For the first time in my life, I actually started to enjoy being in the kitchen. We laughed and talked and tasted, and sometimes dumped things out and started over. And as Joy taught me not to be afraid to try new recipes, I introduced her to my favorite Broadway music, and we sang along together.

Rather than comparing or becoming intimidated by each other's gifts, we learned from each other. As women, it's so easy for someone else's calling to trigger our insecurities. "Pick up a yardstick to measure your life against anyone else's, and you've just picked up a stick and beaten your own soul," Ann Voskamp writes.[5] But in God's plan, our unique callings complement each other beautifully. We become more together than any of us is on our own.

Joy and I and our little crew turned Florida into "home." But it wasn't just about hanging out and having fun. We helped Joy cook meals for new moms in our church and took baked goods to the nursing homes at Christmas. The others cheered me on as I began to teach piano and voice lessons, and eventually started a choir in the youth group. We volunteered together at the community center and worked with the campus outreach. We looked for ways to serve.

Bit by bit, we learned to look for places where God was already working. It became a game. "Guess what I found out about today?" one of the women would often exclaim as she burst through the door on Thursday night. She'd go on to share a specific need she'd seen that we could respond to. Slowly, my "pity poor me" state of mind was replaced by excitement.

Thirty-five years later, Joy is still one of my closest friends. We only lived in the same state for two years, but I still use her recipes and we stay in touch, sharing the latest opportunities God's given us to love and serve in our own communities.

That hot Florida day, John and I really just wanted to take a nap rather than going to that cookout—after all, it wasn't too much to miss. Just cheap hot dogs and hamburgers, right?

Living on purpose isn't just about identifying your gifts and passions, it's also about seeking out other women living with purpose.

THE WOMEN YOU DON'T KNOW (YET!)

Saving money and getting life insurance are responsible investments to make, so we're told. But it's just as critical, if not more, to identify our calling and the areas we want to grow in—spiritually, emotionally, and professionally—and then seek out a mentor to walk with us.

I had no idea how hard it would be to meet people after college. No late-night study breaks to get ice cream or conversations about cute guys as we got ready in the morning. Like all good things in life, building new relationships takes time, energy, and effort.

And where you spend your free time matters. I always encourage my friends who are moving to begin Googling and researching the area long before they pack the truck. Plan. Research. Check it out. Even if you're not moving, the same principle applies.

Be intentional about getting to know people who will build you up. You won't find these sorts of friends, though, if your feet don't take you to the right places. That's why it's so critical to get connected with a church. Sure, not everyone you meet will be mentor material, but you have a greater likelihood of finding a mentor among a group of Christians than at the mall.

Seek out Christian groups and gatherings outside of Sunday morning services, too. Don't limit yourself to just those four walls. Remember, you're looking for other women to share life with. Women you can learn from. Women you want to be like.

Building new connections is a critical step in finding a mentor, and you have to take initiative to seek them out. No excuses! Littlestown, where I grew up, is a tiny dot on the map. And there are amazing women of God there. Keep looking. Keep believing. Keep praying.

Don't sit and sulk, and don't give up. Think about it: if you go to three restaurants and their burgers are subpar, does that mean you become a vegetarian? Of course not! You just do a little bit of research, ask around, and try another place next time.

You may attend a new church one Sunday and walk away rolling your eyes. That's okay. Just don't stop looking. You may hang out with a new acquaintance and leave shaking your head. You'll likely meet many people you don't click well with, but you can learn something from every woman you cross paths with.

It's good to be choosy in your close friendships, and they'll take time to develop and deepen, but it's your responsibility to take the first step and connect. If you want to find a friend, be one! There are a million different ways to meet new people—from planned events like running groups, work gatherings, and book clubs to random "God meetings" that happen at the coffee shop, gym, or grocery store.

Who knows? You may meet a potential mentor as you're waiting to get your oil changed. Or while you're walking your dog. You may have the opportunity to grab lunch with the friend of a friend who lives in the area. Or a business associate you discover a lot in common with. I have met mentors on vacation, at conferences, in theatre productions . . . not just in church.

There is no one formula for connecting with a potential

mentor, but where you take your feet is very important. Where do you hang out? What environments and people are you seeking out? Believe me, neither good friends nor a good mentor will just "happen." So don't merely sit on your couch drinking a smoothie and praying.

Pray, certainly. But then get up and move.

Respond

1. In what ways do you tend to compare yourself with other women? How can you embrace and celebrate your uniqueness and the uniqueness of other women, rather than competing?

2. As you read Joshua's story, how does it encourage you? What wilderness have you experienced in your life—a season that was confusing, disorienting, and discouraging? How does it change your perspective to know that God doesn't waste anything?

3. "Your purpose isn't about making a name for yourself, it's about joining God in the work He is already doing." In what ways is this biblical idea of purpose different from what the world tells you about success? How does this change the way you see your job/career?

4. The smartest thing we can do is come to Jesus just as we are and tell Him we are a sinner who needs a Savior. God loves an authentic confession. Have you said, "No matter what is said by my friends, community, or family, today I choose to be a true follower of Christ"?

5. Where are your feet taking you? How can you be intentional about connecting with other women living with purpose? What new environments can you seek out?

The Courage to Step Out

*You don't have to see the whole
staircase, just take the first step.*

Dr. Martin Luther King Jr.

I'm getting kind of discouraged. I've been here a month now
and I'm really missing meeting with you. I feel so incredibly
alone."

My friend had just accepted a job in Dallas, but we still
kept in touch. "We've been praying for God to bring you a new
mentor," I reminded her. "So how's it going? Have you met
anyone who sticks out to you?"

"Well, there's Caryn, who I met at the church I visited. Yes-
terday, I met Janis at the gym. She seemed really cool and I think
we have a lot in common. And then, you mentioned Linda, who
you know. I have her contact information, but I haven't called her.

"I don't know . . . I'm just so nervous. Finding a mentor is a big deal. What if it's awkward? What if they all say no? Or what if I pick the wrong one?"

"It can feel overwhelming," I acknowledged. "But tell me about the last date you went on."

She was puzzled. "What does that have to do with anything?" She laughed.

"A lot, actually. First dates can be kind of awkward, too. You don't know quite what to expect. Sometimes you have a blast, other times you hold your breath waiting for the evening to be over. But you don't get engaged on your first date—at least I hope not!"

"Huh, you're right." She relaxed a bit. "Maybe I just need to hang out with Caryn and Janis and Linda, get to know them . . . and go from there. After all, here I am stressing out about picking the wrong mentor, and I barely know anything about them."

"Getting connected is a process," I encouraged her. "But we know one thing without a doubt—God's will is for you to do life together with other godly women. To be *known* for who you are. To have someone investing in and nurturing you. God didn't take you all the way to Texas to put you on the shelf. He will go ahead of you and coordinate all the details.

"Your part is just to take the first step. Why not try to meet up with each of the women you mentioned? Don't get desperate and ask some random person to mentor you. Get to know each of them. Listen to their heart and passions. Ask about their God story."

"That's a good reminder," she agreed. "I think I've been so focused on trying to make it happen that I haven't left much room for God. I'm starting to feel less anxious and more excited about this. It's kind of cool to realize that God already knows exactly who my mentor will be."

"Exactly! And I've got a promise for you: 'Trust God from the bottom of your heart; don't try to figure out everything on your own. Listen for God's voice in everything you do, everywhere you go; he's the one who will keep you on track'" (Proverbs 3:5–6 MSG). As we said goodbye, I ached to give her a hug. I was so proud of who she was becoming. And I couldn't wait to see what God had for her!

I feel exactly the same way as I'm writing these words to you. Here we are in chapter 5 already. We've reflected, we've prayed, we've asked God for wisdom . . . now's the time to act.

WHAT HOLDS YOU BACK

Stuck in a small fishing boat in the middle of a storm, the apostles must have been terrified (see Matthew 14:22–36). Huge waves crashed over the side, swamping the boat. The men were terrified and cried out in fear when they saw a figure walking on the water toward them.

And then *it* started talking. But the voice wasn't creepy or foreboding. It was familiar. The wind continued to whip, the waves crashed on, and the boat was on the verge of capsizing.

But somehow, the voice was safe. Calm. Peaceful: "It's me. Don't be afraid."

Peter knew that voice. It was the voice of the man he'd left everything to follow. The voice of Jesus, who just hours before had fed thousands of people with one little boy's lunch. As the overflowing baskets of bread and fish flashed through Peter's mind, he yelled back, "Master, if it's really you, call me to come to you on the water!" (Matthew 14:28 MSG).

"Come ahead," Jesus responded, reaching out His hand.

This was it—now or never. Stay in the boat, and maybe go down with it. Or abandon the little safety he had and step into the craziness of the storm. It defied all reason. I wonder about the other disciples. Did they call Peter crazy? Did they tell him he was seeing things in the fog? Did they try to pull him back?

Here goes nothing! Taking a deep breath, Peter stepped out . . . and his feet didn't sink! His eyes locked on Jesus, he actually walked on top of the water. John Ortberg reminds us, "Hope got Peter out of the boat. Trust held him up. Fear sank him."[1] Everything depends on your focus.

"Lord, save me!" Peter cried out in desperation. And Jesus was there in an instant, pulling him up out of the dark abyss of churning water. Pulling Peter into His embrace, into safety, love, and closer intimacy than ever before.

But it's easy to miss the moment. We all have a boat, you see. Some of our boats are color-coordinated, others painted with flowers or polka dots. Maybe your boat is constantly changing colors, a new splash of paint with every emotion and mood. Or perhaps your hull has been painted over by a dark season in life with brushstrokes of gray and black.

What does your boat look like?

Maybe yours is made of steel, equipped with a GPS and every technological bell and whistle to assure you of a safe and secure ride, just in case God doesn't come through for you. You've christened your ship *On My Own* and boldly set sail!

Perhaps you have a luxury yacht with plush interior. You named her *Cozy and Comfortable*, and as you sit back on the deck with a drink in hand, you think, *Maybe we won't go out to sea. It feels pretty good right here in the harbor.*

Or maybe you own a trim sailboat, dubbed *My Escape*. Hoist

those sails and you'll be whisked away to a remote island where the sun always shines (but doesn't burn you), you've got a private beach, and not a care in the world. At least for the moment.

No matter what ship you sail, we all have one thing in common with the disciples—fear. Maybe they were thinking some of the same things you and I would have been thinking:

"What if it doesn't work and I sink? What will the other guys say about me?"

"Hey. He didn't say my name so I don't have to go."

"No way! Jesus might be able to walk on water, but I sure can't. I'm going to drown."

"Jesus knows I'm afraid. He wouldn't ask me to do anything I'm not comfortable with."

How often do we use this same sort of reasoning when it comes to pursuing a mentor? I've met so many twenty- and thirtysomethings who say to me, "Well, yeah, of course I'd love to have a mentor, but that's never going to happen." They go on to point out valid reasons why:

- The women I do know are all too busy and stressed already with their career or their kids or grandkids. I wouldn't want to burden them.
- I'm nothing special. No one would want to mentor ordinary me. I'm sure they have better things to do with their time.
- It might be awkward, and I wouldn't know what to say. What am I supposed to do—confess my sin? Or recite memory verses? It feels so formal and contrived.
- I'm a private person and I don't trust people easily. I doubt I could open up and share where I'm really at.

What if she gossiped about me?

- I had a mentor once, and it blew up. She acted like a mom—telling me what to do and pressuring and nagging me.
- I'm afraid if I ask someone to mentor me, she'll say no, and then I'll feel stupid. I hate rejection, and I try to avoid it whenever possible.

Don't sell yourself short with any of these excuses. It's easy to focus on all the things that could go wrong, dismiss mentoring because of a negative past experience, or wait for a potential mentor to make the first move. Interestingly, according to a recent study, 82 percent of women agreed that having a mentor was very important, but only 51 percent had actually ever had a mentor.[2] That's a big gap!

If you want something, anything, in life, you have to go out and find it. Create it. Step out of the boat and seek it out, knowing that God will orchestrate all the details. Your mentor most likely won't show up at your front door and introduce herself. In fact, if someone does show up at your door, be suspicious . . . mentoring isn't something to be sold!

I've got news, though. In the same study, 67 percent of women said they had never mentored anyone else because "no one ever asked."[3] As someone who loves to mentor, I am humbled and thrilled when a woman approaches me, but I'm not going to advertise my mentoring services all over social media. I want to meet with women who are intentional in seeking out a relationship, not signing up for a service.

One thing I know, you can't stay in your boat and step into mentoring. Take your pick.

MAKING IT HAPPEN

"I hope that as you engage in the world around you, you'll go for broke in your interactions with people, starting with the ones right in front of you," Bill Hybels writes.[4] Are you ready to go for broke? Why not? We have nothing to lose—and potentially a lot to gain through developing a mentoring relationship!

As we've explored in the last few chapters, the mentoring journey starts with knowing yourself—where you came from, who you are, what you want to move toward in life. This requires slowing down a bit to face your dark side, your fears and insecurities. After all, if you hide from yourself, you can't grow. You'll wake up ten years from now and be the same person.

It's also critical to identify the areas you need to grow in and who you know that excels in that area. Mentoring isn't *just* about deepening your relationship with God. It's about becoming your best you, developing your full potential, so think about all areas of your life where you want to grow—spiritually, emotionally, relationally, and professionally.

For example, a dear friend of mine just got married and her husband was deployed shortly thereafter. Struggling to figure out how to do a marriage long-distance, she decided to look for a mentor who, if possible, is a military wife. Another friend is moving across the country to start her doctorate at a state school. She is seeking out a professor at the university who can help her integrate faith and academics.

When I was starting my dance studio, I looked specifically for a Christian woman to mentor me who had a business background, and as a mom of three young kids, I prayed for God to connect me with a mom whose kids were grown and could help me navigate the craziness of teething, potty-training, and the terrible twos.

What about you? Take a moment to consider where you are in life and list out specific characteristics or traits that you're looking for in a mentor.

Next, take time to evaluate your current connections. Pull out the list of any names you jotted down reading the last few chapters. Perhaps you have someone to add. Think about the women you know or know of. Maybe it's the friend of a friend, a coworker, or an acquaintance. Women who light up the room, who leave you feeling more alive after talking with them. Women who exude wisdom—who are authentic, imperfect, and growing themselves!

If you catch yourself feeling drawn to spend time with her, if the thought pops into your head, *I want to be like her when I "grow up"*—that's a good clue. Step out. Walk across the room. Make the phone call. Ask her out. The worst thing she can say is no.

It can be as simple as, "I'd love to get to know you better and hang out sometime. Would you be willing to grab lunch sometime or meet for coffee?" You can also add something more personal to your situation like, "I'm new in town and am trying to get connected" or "I really admire your walk with God" or "I feel like I could learn so much from you."

Have a couple days and times available to connect with the woman you're asking out, but don't ask her to be your mentor just yet. Don't jump in front of God, but if you can, do offer to pay for her coffee or meal. After all, she's taken time out of her day to meet with you, so be sure to value and appreciate her intentionality and time.

As you spend time together, be yourself. Relax. This is not a job interview; this is getting to know each other. No masks—let her see the real you! One of the biggest misconceptions about mentoring is that it is formal and contrived, when that is the furthest thing from the truth.

So sip coffee. Go for a walk together. Laugh. Share your stories, your struggles, your dreams. Remember, whether this woman goes on to officially mentor you or not, this conversation—this moment—is a gift. Enjoy it! And ask God for wisdom.

A RISK WORTH TAKING

Patty radiated joy, and there wasn't a fake bone in her body. As we chatted after church, we realized we lived in the same neighborhood, only five minutes apart. And we were both looking for a walking buddy. Patty seemed like the real deal, and I couldn't wait to get to know her better. So we started walking every Wednesday at 8 a.m., after my kids were off to school.

The temperature was just right at that time of morning, and our friendship quickly took off. Some days I cried as I shared how overwhelmed I felt. How frustrated and lonely I was. Patty was there. She listened. She didn't call me crazy or tell me to get over it. But Patty also didn't let me wallow in the doldrums either. She helped me walk out the truth of who God was for me and how He would see me through.

All along, Patty had been right under my nose—she sat right in front of me at church for months before we talked. If I hadn't been looking and curious, willing to take a chance and try, I never would have discovered a workout buddy, friend, mentor.

Do you have the courage to take a chance in order to grow? It's ironic, come to think of it. Many of us take out thousands of dollars in student debt to get a degree that, in the end, may have little correlation with our job. Repayments are the last thing from comfortable or fun, but someone along the way told us that going to college was part of growing up.

Finding a mentor is so much easier. And I would argue it's just as important to your growth, if not more, than having a BS or MA after your name. I am thrilled to be part of a church that has made mentoring a priority and plugs twenty- and thirty-somethings in to meet one-on-one with someone more seasoned. But not all churches do. Most likely, you will have to take action to pursue a mentor for yourself. And you can.

One of my favorite action verses is from Ezra 10:4: "Rise up; this matter is in your hands. . . . so take courage and do it." I often challenge myself with these words when I'm stepping into something new. New is scary. New is overwhelming. New is awkward. And new is exciting! But just about everything in life requires some level of risk. From dating to new roommates to switching jobs to going back to school to getting married to having kids. You get the idea. Helen Keller points out, "Life is either a daring adventure or nothing at all."[5]

Fear—it's at the core of every reason that holds you back from pursuing a mentor. Fear of rejection. Fear of failure. Fear of feeling stupid. Fear of not being understood. What are your fears about connecting with a potential mentor?

Who do you know that you can ask to coffee or lunch this week? The pressure's off! All you have to do is show up, step out, and see what connections God makes. He's calling you to leave your boat behind. To step into a new space of confidence, trust, and growth.

Sure, there's fear. Sure, there's risk. Will you take the leap anyway?

Respond

1. What does your boat look like? Take a few minutes to draw your boat (stick figures are fine!) and christen her with a name that describes where you're at.

2. Peter had the courage to trust Jesus and step out of the boat into the unknown. What holds you back? What fears do you have about connecting with a mentor? Are you willing to give up comfort in order to grow?

3. "If you want something, anything, in life, you have to go out and find it. Step out of your boat and seek it out, knowing that God will orchestrate all the details." Can you think of a time when you intentionally sought something out? How did God show up?

4. What have you learned about yourself so far as you've read this book? What areas do you want to grow in? Who do you know that excels in that area? How can you be strategic about what you're looking for in a mentor?

5. Identify one woman you can ask out this week. What is the most natural environment for both of you (coffee, lunch, going for a walk, meeting at her house or yours, etc.)? Take a moment to talk with God about it, remembering that He is going ahead of you.

6

Popping the Question with Confidence

*Instead of waiting for someone to take
you under their wing, go out and find
a good wing to climb under.*

Dave Thomas

very time we get together, I walk away so encouraged and challenged. I'm curious . . . would you be willing to mentor me? I'm facing a lot of big decisions coming up, and I need wisdom and godly input."

I love watching God work. From dating, to her job, to new ministry opportunities, my friend's life was changing at break-neck speed. She had so much to offer the world.

And here she was asking me to walk with her? What a privilege!

"I'd be honored," I responded excitedly. "A few things you should know about me, though: I'm not perfect, I don't have all the answers, and my biggest asset I can share with you is helping you connect with God in a new way."

"That makes two of us," she answered. "I don't want a mentor who has her act all together and pops out her wisdom like a Pez dispenser. Believe me, I've already experienced that with another person. She just talked my ear off! Giving me advice and telling me what to do . . . it was *her* way or the highway.

"I'm really looking for a safe place to be me . . . to talk out what I'm thinking and feeling. I feel like there's so much spinning around in my head, and my journal can only fit so much. I've been praying for God to connect me with a woman to listen, pray with me, and help me seek out God's will."

We went on to discuss the particulars of time and place. Our schedules matched up for Tuesday mornings, so we decided to plan for coffee at 8 a.m. at the Starbucks near her work.

Now, on to the fun stuff! Whenever I begin to mentor another woman, I want to know where *she* is at in life and what she wants to move toward. So I ask a lot of questions (but not in rapid-fire fashion): "Where are you stuck? Where do you need wisdom? How can I best help and support you? What would you like to see change in your relationship with God?"

It does me little good to impose my ideas—after all, I'm still getting to know her. My job is to listen and seek to understand. To get past surface issues to the heart of the matter. To nurture her as a fellow sister in Christ and really help her thrive.

"Hmm . . . You're really making me think! Sometimes, all I see are my flaws and insecurities. It's a constant string of thoughts that I can't shake free of: *You're not enough. You'll never be enough. You're so pitiful, why even try to change?* But the other day my friend posted this quote, and it made me stop and think:

'Maybe this year, to balance the list, we ought to walk through the rooms of our lives . . . not looking for flaws, but for potential.'[1] Can you help me with that?"

"Oh, there's nothing that would make me more excited!" I reached across the table to grab her hand. And so our journey began.

TEN KEY THINGS TO LOOK FOR IN A MENTOR

You've made a date with a potential mentor, whether it's coffee, dinner, or taking a walk. Now what? As you meet this gal and get to know her, keep an eye out for these key traits:

A good listener. A good mentor is not a preacher; she's a companion on the journey. As you meet with her, does she listen, ask questions, and draw you out? Does she take time to understand you? Or does she jump too quickly to offer you *her* advice?

Someone you connect with. Don't overlook the importance of personality—yours and hers. Do you tend to be drawn to people who are outgoing and high energy or more introverted and reflective? There's no need to force a relationship with someone you don't click with.

Safe and trustworthy. Judgment, criticism, and gossip will sabotage a mentoring relationship faster than anything. Do you feel comfortable talking with this woman and "dumping your truck"? Or does she have a reputation of passing along so-called prayer requests?

Imperfect, but growing. The best mentor is a woman who is constantly challenging herself and pursuing growth in her own life. She's not content with the status quo, and she doesn't put on masks. Is she down-to-earth and real, or does she seem a little too perfect?

A woman of authentic faith. There's nothing more refreshing than someone who doesn't just believe in God, but walks with Him day-to-day. Does she love and follow Jesus? Does she have a growing relationship with God, or is she just going through the motions?

Living on purpose. If you want to discover your purpose, you need to do it with a woman who is passionate and thriving. Does the gal you're sitting with know who she is and what God created her for? Can she say no when necessary, or is she a people pleaser?

A role model. Mentoring is not about becoming a mini version of your mentor. God has created each of us wonderfully unique. At the same time, think about whom you want to emulate. Does she have the character, knowledge, and skills that you desire for your own life?

Speaks the truth in love. We all need a cheerleader, but a mentor is more than just that. Is she willing to tell you the truth and give you honest feedback, even when it's hard to hear? (And are you willing to listen and prayerfully consider her insight?)

Sees your potential. Pick a mentor who you know has your best interest in mind; someone you can trust to bring you back to God's Word, not just to her own opinions. Is she into herself, or is she focused on empowering you to become the woman God created you to be?

A life-giving relationship. Despite the differences between you and a potential mentor, when you spend time together, do you feel more alive? More in tune with God? Do you gain clarity and focus in life? Do you think, *We could have kept talking?* These are good clues.

I can't think of a better word to describe mentoring than *nurture*. The dictionary defines it: "to encourage somebody or something to grow, develop, thrive and be successful."[2] Many of the women I talk with who've had a negative mentoring experience didn't take the time to get to know their mentor beforehand and consider if she was a good fit. Instead, they got desperate and asked the first woman who came along. So don't jump before you talk to God about it.

Look for a woman who will help you blossom and grow.

I love how Susan Hunt summarizes the mentoring journey: "A woman possessing faith and spiritual maturity enters into a nurturing relationship with a younger woman in order to encourage and equip her to live for God's glory."[3] *That* is what we're after.

HOW TO EASILY ASK A POTENTIAL MENTOR

Her face beamed as she walked across the room where the conference was held, supporting her husband as he walked with two canes. She appeared to be in her mid-sixties, yet energetic and full of life. She was confident but not haughty. Calm and centered but bubbling over with sheer joy. *Who is she?* I was captivated, drawn to her like a magnet. *What is her story?*

The next day, I was standing in line for lunch, scrolling through my phone, when I realized she was right behind me. Here was my moment! It was now or never. My heart beating fast, I turned to introduce myself and we struck up a conversation.

We missed half of the afternoon's activities, sharing our hearts long after our turkey sandwiches were gone. Turns out, her husband Allen was a Vietnam vet who'd lost both legs in the war. Linda's first husband died from cancer, and as she was grieving and healing, God brought Allen into her life as a trusted friend. Little did she know that after ten years, God would open her heart to love again and she'd become Allen's wife.

"Your story is such an inspiration," I said, encouraging her. "You just exude the Lord and you have so much wisdom. I would love to stay in touch. I know it'd have to be long distance . . . but can we be friends? Will you mentor me?" It all came tumbling out in one conversation, despite my better judgment. (I didn't even follow my own guideline of never asking a stranger to be a mentor!)

Her eyes lit up. "I would love to, Jayme! Let's definitely stay in touch."

Every mentoring relationship looks a little bit different. Some are face-to-face, others long distance. Some are for life, others God sends to get us through a tough season. "Mentors come to us in the most unlikely forms, and when we most need them," John Schlimm reflects.[4]

I couldn't agree more! One thing is for certain, though: a potential mentor can't read your mind. After you've spent time getting to know each other and prayed about it, if you believe this woman is a good fit . . . well, it's time to pop the question. Don't ask her over text or email. Schedule another date, sit down face-to-face, and then go for it.

- **Share what you admire about her.** Why are you asking her to be your mentor? For example, "You live passionately—like you know exactly who God created you to be" or "I'm drawn to your confidence and wisdom. I want to become more like that" or "You are a woman of faith and your relationship with God is so alive."

- **Be honest about where you want to grow:** "I so easily get caught up in people pleasing and have a hard time saying no" or "I need wisdom and discernment in making some big decisions" or "I want to move closer to God but don't know how." Your willingness to be honest here will set the stage for the tone of your relationship.

- **Invite her to mentor you:** "I'm tired of trying to figure life out on my own. Would you be willing to mentor me? To share your wisdom and insight?" Don't coerce, beg, or force yourself on her. *Ask.* Remember, God has already gone ahead of you and it's up to Him to make the connection. Your job is to be bold, take the risk, and ask.

- **State your expectations:** Be specific. "I'm not looking for a counselor or a mom, but someone who will help me think things through and push me to grow." Explain that you've been praying to connect with a woman who sees your potential and will walk with you in becoming the woman God created you to be.

BAM! Just like that, you did it. Asking someone to be your mentor isn't hard. What's hard is the fear of rejection. The fear of being vulnerable. The fear of making the wrong decision.

Step out anyway. In life and in relationships, you'll never get what you don't ask for. You can hang out with someone informally for years, but asking a woman to be your mentor speaks to the value you hope to gain and shows her you take the relationship seriously.

WHAT IF SHE SAYS NO?

Your worst fears come true. She graciously declines, citing busyness or not feeling equipped to be a mentor or any other number of reasons. Understandably, you're disappointed. Maybe even mad at God. After all, you've prayed about this. You sought God. You took a risk to ask, and the door slammed in your face.

If God really wants me to have a mentor, why would He do this to me? you wonder. Don't throw in the towel on mentoring just yet! I am confident that every no means God has a better yes . . . but you may not see it yet.

Perhaps you got too gung-ho about finding a mentor and ran ahead of God. Relax, slow down your pace a bit, and remember what is true: "No good thing [including a mentor!] does he withhold from those who walk uprightly" (Psalm 84:11 ESV). Keep walking in God's paths with your eyes wide open. Don't give up. Or it may also be that the woman you asked was a great fit . . . but she wasn't ready. Don't personalize—her no may likely have nothing to do with you. You didn't say or do something wrong. You want a mentor who is in tune with God, so if she is preoccupied with other commitments or priorities at the moment, the timing's just not right.

Though mentoring is prioritized in business and academic settings, churches tend to focus more on small groups and Bible studies. I'll never forget when I asked Tracey to mentor me. She was a women's leader at church and I'd always looked up to her. Tracey invited me to lunch to talk more, but I was surprised to find four other women already sitting at the table with her.

"Jayme, have a seat. I'm so glad you could make it!" She greeted me with a smile.

I tried to hide my disappointment as I looked through the menu. I was hoping for some one-on-one time to share my heart, not a ladies' luncheon. Tracey went on to share how we'd all approached her about mentoring, and since she had a very busy schedule, she thought the best thing would be to get together every few months to catch up and encourage one another.

"That's a great idea!" one of the other women responded. "I have a lot going on this fall, so maybe we should try for Christmas. This restaurant is decorated so nice at Christmastime!"

My heart sank as I realized that my tablemates and I had two very different ideas of mentoring. Don't get me wrong, I've hosted gatherings in my home and I always look forward to quality girl time with other women! But when I am seeking out a mentor, my prayer is for a safe and confidential relationship, meeting privately with a woman who is willing to invest in me. It's okay—it's good—to be picky about the mentor you choose, and assertive about what you're looking for.

Tracey had a different vision, and that's okay. It just wasn't what I needed at that time. I was disappointed. I thought for sure that Tracey would be my next mentor. Key word: *I*. I was so focused on what I wanted that I totally missed God on this one.

I wanted to go grab a pint of Ben and Jerry's, curl up in my bed, and sing along with Eeyore, "Nobody wants to be my [mentor], what's a [girl] to do?" But I knew that wouldn't fix anything. So I cried out to God, "I know it's Your will for me to be in a mentoring relationship. Please show me who You want me to ask. Bring her into my life . . . and the sooner the better!"

And in that moment, God brought to mind Matthew 7:7: "Ask and it will be given to you; seek and you will find; knock and the door will be opened to you." The verb implies "continue"

—continue asking, continue seeking, continue knocking. Rest assured, there's not just one mentor out there for you. Over the course of your life, I pray that God will bring many women across your path that you will learn and grow with.

So ask . . . and keep on asking. Seek . . . and keep on seeking. Knock . . . and keep looking for doors to knock on.

A HUNDRED-MILE JOURNEY

Am I going crazy? Did I really see an angel? Was I dreaming? Reeling with the news that she was pregnant with the Messiah, Mary struggled to make sense of it (see Luke 1:26–56).

For nothing is impossible with God. Those words, her only hope in a world coming unraveled. *I'll be the laughingstock of Nazareth. People will mock me, shun me . . . and what about my beloved Joseph? Will he understand? Or will he leave me too?*

Confusion. Questions. Excitement. Fear. Anticipation. I imagine her brain was about to burst! But Mary remembered the angel's words: "Even Elizabeth your relative is going to have a child in her old age . . ." (verse 36).

Elizabeth. It's likely that Mary didn't know her cousin well. Elizabeth lived in the hill country of Judah, close to a hundred miles away from Nazareth. But Mary knew she needed help and support, and she didn't waste any time. Packing her bags, she started the trek. Her journey wasn't easy, safe, or fun.

We don't know if Mary traveled with a caravan or walked the hundred miles on foot, but regardless, it would have taken her, at a minimum, four to five long, sweaty, blister-filled days. Along the way, she could have been taken captive by bandits, raped, or attacked by wild animals.

It was a hard journey in itself, let alone absorbing the news the angel had given her. No warm fuzzy feelings about following God's plan. I imagine Mary was just trying to put one foot in front of the other. She spent the better part of an entire week plodding across the hot, dusty plains of Israel. Sometimes, finding a mentor takes time and energy, too.

You may not walk a hundred miles across a desert to find your mentor, but you certainly may endure some discomfort, some nos, some discouragement along the way. You may not have an angel appear to you, but listen for the prompting of the Holy Spirit, nudging you out of your comfort zone—to walk across the room, build a new relationship, and ask.

"God has blessed you." Elizabeth's words must have been such an encouragement. "You are blessed because you believed that the Lord would do what he said" (Luke 1:42–45 NLT).

Mary risked everything to seek out a woman who could help her navigate this scary, new chapter in her life. I imagine they discussed the angel's visit, the what-ifs of life with or without Joseph, the how-tos of delivering a child, parenting, being a wife, cooking, and so much more. There was nothing Mary couldn't ask Elizabeth.

That's the nature of a mentoring relationship—there's nothing you can't discuss, no question off-limits. Because for every struggle you face in life, God longs to give you guidance, support, wisdom, and encouragement.

Take it from Mary. Sometimes the road to finding a mentor can be awkward, difficult, or discouraging, but the walk is well worth the distance. How far are you willing to walk?

Respond

1. What specific characteristics and traits are you looking for in a mentor? Take a minute to jot them down. You can refer to the list in this chapter, but make sure to add your own, too!

2. When you hear the word *nurture*, what words and images come to your mind? How does understanding that mentoring = nurturing other women broaden your perspective on what this relationship might look like for you? Is there someone you'd like to ask to mentor you?

3. How would you handle it if she said no? What insecurities and negative thoughts might this trigger? Write out several promises from Scripture that can encourage you to keep on seeking and asking, rather than giving up.

4. Where do you see yourself in Mary's story? What might it look like for you to go the extra mile as you look for a mentor? Where do you need to trust God and wait patiently?

5. Press "pause" on your mentor search for just a minute. Calm your heart. Listen for the prompting of the Holy Spirit. How can you move forward with wisdom, rather than desperately throwing yourself out there, asking every woman you meet to mentor you?

Section Three

Growing Together

7

I Have a Mentor . . . Now What?

Mentoring is a brain to pick, an ear to listen, and a push in the right direction.

JOHN CROSBY

To be honest, I'm a little hesitant about this whole mentoring thing. I got burnt pretty bad before, so it's hard for me to open up sometimes," my friend shared.

Right from the get-go, I appreciated her honesty. Her willingness to own her fears.

"My church started a mentoring program with five or six teenage girls in each subgroup. Our leader encouraged us that nothing was off-limits—frustrations, struggles, questions. I was relieved because I'd really been struggling, and didn't know who to talk to about it.

"'This is a safe place,' our mentor reassured us. 'What you say here stays here.'

"Over the first several weeks, I shared with the group that

I was really insecure about my weight, and that some days I couldn't even stand to look in the mirror.

"I opened up about my crush on Luke. How I desperately wanted to go out with him, and how angry I was at my parents because they wouldn't let me because I was 'too young.'

"I admitted that I'd been doubting God a lot, too. Was He real? Did He care about me?

"Surprisingly, the girls didn't make weird faces or laugh at me. I felt heard. Understood. Known. *Wow, this really is a safe place!* Or so I thought. One night when I got home, my parents called me in to the living room.

"'You are in big trouble, young lady,' my dad snapped. Turns out, my mentor had been funneling back to Mom and Dad every single last thing I said in group. I was livid."

"I vowed to never make *that* mistake again," she told me. "I took the word *mentor* out of my vocabulary. I'm okay with friends, but a mentor? It still leaves a bad taste in my mouth."

"I'm so sorry." I felt her pain—the pain of broken trust. And I was angry to see the power of mentoring so misused and exploited. "I'm proud of you, though, for taking the risk to reach out anyway and connect again."

"Yeah." She continued, "I didn't for a while. But then I figured, what the heck! I'm done trying to be tough and figure out life on my own. I need somebody to walk with me and remind me of the truth. So I'm giving mentoring another chance. I've been praying for God to give me wisdom, and maybe you are the answer to my prayers."

"Well, I'm far from perfect," I assured her with a smile. "But my desire is that when we meet it's a safe place to dump your truck, as I call it. We can talk about anything—wherever you're at. And it stays between you, me, and God. It's never my intention to hurt you in any way, but if something is bothering you, can you let me know? I'm still learning and growing too."

I'm always amazed at how good God is, instilling hope for a fresh start. And it's true for you, too . . . no matter what your mentoring baggage.

GIVING VOICE TO YOUR INSECURITIES

I'd been a Microsoft girl for years, so I was definitely charting new territory when I bought a MacBook Pro. And I'm not exactly the queen of tech savvy, so I was thrilled to hear about the One to One program that Apple offers: "One to One will help you do more than you ever thought possible with your Mac," their website explains. "Get a full hour of uninterrupted time to work one-on-one with a trainer on the topic of your choice."[1]

Why not? I figured. I made the appointment online and showed up at the Apple store a few minutes early, excited and nervous. I had a list of questions written out, but my brain was spinning. Thankfully, Bethany was the perfect trainer. She didn't make fun of me for my lack of knowledge. She took time to answer my many questions. Before I knew it, we were laughing and having a good time . . . and I was learning a lot too.

We spent an hour exploring all the facets of a Mac—customizing my desktop display, setting up iCloud, exploring Keynote, Final Cut Pro, and iPhoto. Bethany even showed me how to sync all of my email addresses under the Mail app on my iPhone and taught me about using Bluetooth to transfer files. My mind was blown. I had discovered a gold mine! It would have taken me months, if not years, to figure all this out on my own.

∽

"Come back and see me anytime," Bethany encouraged me. "I'll be here for you!"

I left the Mac store that day with a skip in my step, excited to apply all that I had learned. Bethany had explained the technical language that looked like gibberish in the 144-page user's guide, giving me the tools and confidence to use my Mac for things I'd never dreamed of.

And then it hit me . . . this is mentoring at its finest. We tend to learn and grow best—whether it's in our computer knowledge or our relationship with God—in the context of a personal relationship. Not just reading a book or watching an online tutorial or sermon.

As you start your mentoring relationship, you may find crazy irrational thoughts going through your head. Satan may attack you with feeling inadequate, broken, busy, or not worthy. But it's not just you—most likely your mentor is struggling with similar feelings.

You may think *I can't open up to her! If she really knew me at my core, she would certainly walk away or give up on me!* At the same time, your mentor is worrying *I'm not good enough to mentor her; I'm not sure I even have what it takes!*

You may think *I don't need any help* or *I'm too busy*, while your mentor gets sucked into believing *I'm not equipped to meet her needs . . . maybe it's too big of a commitment.*

You may think, *I've made too many mistakes. I don't think I can ever get out of this rut.* Your mentor wonders, *Am I worthy to guide someone else when my own life has been so messy?*

Doubt. Insecurity. Uncertainty. Fear. Lies. Excuses. Satan knows full well the transformative power of mentoring, and he will do anything in his power to sabotage it. Don't buy it. You see, the very fears and insecurities that cause you to shut down and pull away can do just the opposite too—they can connect you and your mentor in a powerful way.

So why not bring up the conversation? Ask your mentor, What are you most reticent or unsure about when it comes to mentoring me? And share your fears too. You may find you have more in common than you realize. Honesty is the best antidote to the rip current of lies and insecurities that will suck you out to sea.

MENTORING THAT FITS YOUR LIFESTYLE

Mentoring is so much more than just an appointment on your calendar—it's a way of life. Whatever season you're in and no matter what your schedule looks like, you can tailor mentoring to your lifestyle. There's no one "right" place or time or structure that you must conform to, but here are a few things to consider as you get started:

Where to meet. One of my coauthor Laura's most profound mentoring experiences while we've been writing together happened on a ski trip. She'd been wrestling through a major decision, and the ski trip gave her the opportunity to think out loud and get feedback.

"It was amazing," Laura shared with me. "Each ride up on the ski lift, I talked with my mentor and listened to her input. And as I skied down each slope, I prayed and soaked up the beauty of God's creation. Our day together was just what I needed—both time to talk out my fears and time to reflect and listen to God."

You can meet with your mentor for coffee or a meal. You can go walking or running together, that is, if you can talk while you run (I wish I could!). If you have little ones, you can invite your mentor to your home or meet at the park so the kids can play while you talk. You can go to your mentor's home (particularly if she has a big front porch or a hot tub)!

You can cook together, or serve in the community. You can garden together in the spring, go berry picking or to the local market in the summer, have a picnic in the fall, or assemble food baskets around the holidays. Maybe you're a runner and your mentor is not. That's okay. Look for things you have in common and experiences you can share. Think outside the box!

What to avoid. As a foodie, I'm always excited to visit a new local restaurant when I meet with someone, but I've learned my lesson the hard way here. Once, we arrived to find that the café actually wasn't opening for a few more weeks—oops—back to the drawing board! And then there was our brilliant idea to meet at a lunch spot right next to my friend's work. The only problem? We kept getting interrupted by her coworkers who apparently all ate lunch there too.

As you are creative, consider the best environment to have an intentional and authentic conversation. Try to stay away from noisy public places—you don't want to be yelling at each other over the music! Also, be wary of spots with too many distractions. It will be hard to stay focused and talk honestly if you bump into people you know. The same is true if you're constantly checking your phone.

Coffee shops are one of my favorite meeting spots, especially on rainy or cold days, but make sure to look for a quiet corner or a semiprivate table. You may feel less comfortable sharing your heart if someone you know is standing in line to order just a few feet away!

For these reasons, I've become a big fan of nonconventional meeting spots, so don't limit yourself to restaurants and coffee shops. Every meeting can't be a grand adventure, but getting out of your normal space does wonders to bring a fresh perspective on life.

When to meet. This one is totally up to you and your mentor. Compare your schedules and look for overlap in free time. Some of the gals I meet with prefer to grab coffee in the morning before work; others pack a lunch and meet me at the park. Whether it's morning, afternoon, or evening, make sure to respect your mentor's time. Don't ask her to revolve around your schedule, and avoid making last-minute changes. Try to arrive a few minutes early and be present in the moment, rather than thinking about everything else you have to do that day.

Your mentor is setting aside her time to invest in you when she could be doing a million other things, so be flexible and considerate, not entitled and demanding. You may need to juggle a few things in your schedule—if her only free time is in the evenings, skip your workout that day or get up early to exercise. Or see if she'd be willing to go walking or jogging with you.

You likely have a job or a family or a thousand other commitments . . . and so does your mentor. So use your time wisely! There's no hard-and-fast rule for how often or how long to meet, but I suggest planning for an hour once a week or every other week. That way, you won't spend the majority of your meeting just catching up on life. You'll be able to go deep, share where you're stuck and struggling, ask for godly input, and pray together.

Even as I'm writing this, I don't want to give you a list of steps to follow, because mentoring is a relationship, not A + B = C. Remember this: If it works for you and your mentor, it works.

Don't make scheduling more complicated than it needs to be. Talk with your mentor and collaborate together to create a plan that works for both of you.

Every single mentoring relationship I've had over the last thirty-five years has been a bit different, because every two people are unique. And your needs and preferences will likely change, too, with each season of your life. So be creative—the sky's the limit!

MORE THAN GOOD INTENTIONS

I'm a procrastinator when it comes to packing for a trip. I don't usually start until the night before, so I rush through Target ten minutes before they close to pick up sandals and sunscreen and anything else I can think of. And the problem with starting laundry at midnight is that I either have to stay awake to put each load in the dryer or risk packing still-damp clothes.

But sometimes I pay the price for my good intentions without a plan. There's nothing worse than getting to the beach and realizing you've forgotten your swimsuit. Or arriving at the airport and reaching for your passport, only to remember you left it on your dresser.

Whether you're headed to catch the sun in Florida or explore the streets of Italy, any vacation requires preparation. You have to ask off of work, reserve a place to stay, fill your car with gas, maybe even find a dog sitter. Skip any one of these, and your trip won't end well. The same is true of mentoring. You may be able to wing it in some areas of your life, but not here.

So what do you say to your mentor now that you have one?

I tend to shy away from hyper-organized or short-term mentoring programs that rely on an outline of questions or a specific agenda for each session. (Yet when new programs are just getting started, having guidelines can certainly be helpful. You might, for example, go through the Respond section at the end of each chapter in this book.) Too much structure will kill the authenticity. At the same time, here are some key habits to help you cultivate a healthy mentoring relationship:

Be authentic and take off your mask. A mentor is someone you can talk to about absolutely anything without embarrassment or fear. It's not testifying in court or going to confession. So don't try to impress her. Sure, it will take a bit of time for you to get to know each other, but remember why you're here. Take time to reflect on, talk out, and pray together about where you're at and what you want to move toward. This is a safe place to dump your truck!

Be prepared and take it seriously. Pray and maybe even write out what you want to discuss with your mentor before you meet. Be brave enough to ask your mentor the questions that plague you at night—whether it's about dating and relationships, building your business, going back to school, how to get your little one to go to sleep, making a career change, doubting God . . . you name it. Identify where you want to grow. Harness this opportunity!

Be teachable and willing to be challenged. Humility is critical. Admit where you don't have life figured out. Ask for input and godly advice. Proverbs says, "Without good direction, people lose their way . . . Take good counsel and accept correction—that's the way to live wisely and well" (Proverbs 11:14, 19:20 MSG). A mentoring relationship will create movement in your life—motivating you to go after what God has placed in your heart, no matter what the obstacles.

Be open to the Holy Spirit. You likely won't agree with everything your mentor says, and that's okay. She isn't perfect; she's a companion on the journey. Learn from your mentor's stories, life experience, and mistakes. Take in her input and pray about it. Mentoring is ultimately about getting closer to God and discovering His purpose for your life, not becoming a mini version of your mentor. She is there for support, but she can't replace God in your life!

Be respectful and grateful. Mentoring is not a one-way street. You respect her time, she respects yours. You listen and seek to understand, just as she does for you. Take time to get to know and care about her—not just what she can do for you. Never take your mentor for granted. Thank her for investing in you! The day will come when you have the opportunity to pass on what you've learned by mentoring someone else.

Be face-to-face. With today's technology, you can certainly communicate with your mentor over tools like FaceTime or Skype, especially if one of you relocates. But I believe that nothing can replace a real, live face-to-face conversation. "Though I have much to write to you, I would rather not use paper and ink," John said. "Instead I hope to come to you and talk face to face, that our joy may be complete" (2 John 1:12 ESV). Face-to-face is the best way to grow!

Be intentional about the relationship you're building. Mentoring isn't magic . . . you'll get out of it what you put into it. Don't just add it to your calendar like your chiropractic appointment or paying your rent. Don't make it an obligation. This is an incredible opportunity. You get to spend time with a woman who's likely been there and done that when it comes to what you're thinking and feeling as a twenty- or thirtysomething.

FOLLOW WISELY, DO LIFE TOGETHER

I am not a giver-upper! The snow began to fall thick and fast as the kids and I hit the road to visit my parents in Pennsylvania, but I forged ahead hoping for the best. Soon I could barely see a car's length in front of me. A million terrifying scenarios played through my mind . . . being stranded on the side of the road, or worse, careening off the slippery asphalt. Praying for God to protect us, despite my poor decision making, I noticed an 18-wheeler just ahead of us.

Stay in his tire tracks. I wasn't sure if it was God talking to me or just my own thoughts, but I didn't dismiss it. If God can speak through a donkey and a burning bush, a truck isn't too far out of the ordinary, is it? Carefully maneuvering the minivan across the snowy lanes, my hands gripped the wheel with determination. Tires spinning, the back end began to fishtail to the left. *Bump bump.* The tires regained traction as they came in contact with the packed snow, and we all breathed a sigh of relief.

I could've tried to follow a lot of different vehicles, but the cars around me were swerving and spinning out, just trying to stay on the road. The truck driver, though, could see what was up ahead from his vantage point in the cab. His taillights were a bright beacon in the darkness, and his tire tracks packed down the drifts. This obviously wasn't his first snowstorm! When the truck braked, I braked. I anticipated the curves and hills ahead by following his lead.

Similarly, your mentor is "someone whose hindsight can

become your foresight."[2] In the blizzards of life, your mentor can shed the light of God's truth on your path, keeping you on track with God's purpose when confusion and doubt hamper your visibility. But being mentored isn't hooking yourself up to a tow truck and going along with "whatever." Unquestioned submission and dependence is the furthest thing from genuine growth! The truck broke the wind, but I had to maintain control of my car, letting off the gas and taking turns slowly to avoid sliding.

The road conditions progressively worsened over the next half hour, and I finally pulled off at a somewhat sketchy motel. I was shaking, afraid, and grateful. We were able to get one of the last rooms available. The next morning, the news reported the story that could have been ours. The interstate was impassable because of the blizzard, and hundreds of people were still stranded in their cars. A chill swept through me as I realized our narrow escape.

That snowy night, I could have forged ahead on my own, bragging about my new tires and reasoning, *Why do I need to follow someone else's taillights? My car's beams are just fine!* Thank God I didn't try to do it alone. "Follow my example, as I follow the example of Christ," Paul admonished those he mentored (1 Corinthians 11:1). This isn't a mindless following, but an intentional choice to spend time with people who will shape and grow us to be more like Jesus.

"They had been with Jesus." It's the first thing people noticed about the disciples (Acts 4:13 ESV). This core group ate with Jesus, walked the dusty roads of Galilee together, served alongside of Jesus, and asked a lot of questions. They did life together.

Joanna sticks out as an unlikely disciple, though. A high-ranking woman in Herod's court, she was surprisingly quite close to Jesus. This brave gal was with Jesus to the very end at the cross, and she was one of the three women who discovered the empty tomb (Luke 24:10).

Yet Joanna, unlike some of the other disciples, wasn't with Jesus all the time. Due to her husband's role managing the royal court, she most certainly had responsibilities to attend to. Joanna lived and worked in a setting that was completely anti-Jesus. She most likely met many well-to-do and famous people who came to visit Herod, yet Joanna intentionally chose to follow Jesus, even when it wasn't popular, convenient, or easy.

What drove Joanna? The Bible doesn't tell us all the details, but we do know this: Jesus healed her of some kind of disease or ailment (Luke 8:1–3). We don't know if it was a physical, mental, or emotional illness. We just know she got a fresh start! And you can too.

You can't see your mentor every day, and unless you go camping together, it's doubtful you'll fall asleep watching the night sky, like Jesus and some of the disciples did. You can't be together 24/7. Like Joanna, each of us has daily tasks to attend to, but a mentor who is following Jesus herself can offer a new perspective on your storms and help you make wise decisions.

I wonder . . . What are your prayers and hopes as you start walking with your mentor? Take a few moments to journal this out and talk with God. Come to Him with no agenda—just open yourself up to be changed and transformed.

"I am making all things new," Jesus promises—and that includes you (Revelation 21:5 ESV). God is just around the bend. His light shines even farther than your mentor can see from her vantage point. And He's present with you right now, too, longing to grow and heal you just like He did Joanna. Will you follow Him?

Respond

1. Have you had to adjust your thinking when your mentor doesn't tell you what you want to hear? What insecurities and irrational thoughts are you struggling with? Do you feel inadequate, broken, too busy, not worthy—or something else?

2. List three topics you hope to discuss with your mentor. How can you make mentoring fit your lifestyle (consider day, time, location, etc.)? Be creative! The sky's the limit!

3. In what ways can you be intentional about the new relationship you are building, rather than just going through the motions? Identify at least one key habit that you want to build into your mentoring relationship . . . and your friendships, too!

4. Like Joanna, do you find yourself in situations where it isn't popular, convenient, or easy to follow Jesus? How do you navigate this? How can you integrate your faith with your day-to-day life?

5. "Your mentor is a gift, but she can never replace God in your life." How can you be intentional about building spiritual disciplines and intimacy with God into your life, rather than idolizing your mentor?

8

Navigating Conflict

*Beautiful light is born of darkness, so the faith
that springs from conflict is often the strongest.*

R. Turnbull

"I just don't understand why this is such a big deal!" She was annoyed with me, that I could tell. My friend hoped I would encourage her to go for it and get back in the dating scene, but she'd just come out of a difficult breakup, and I was worried about her.

"Really take time to consider your motives," I encouraged her. "Are you champing at the bit to go on a date because you're trying to numb out? Unless you take time to really process your pain and forgive your ex, you'll likely drag all of that into your next relationship."

Walking with your mentor is not all roses and sunshine. She's not just your cheerleader and encourager, she's also an adviser. A good mentor will tell you what you *need* to hear, which is not always the same as what you *want* to hear.

"I understand that you're lonely," she may say. "Believe me, I've been there! But is it really worth compromising your values just so you can fit in?"

"Have you ever considered that maybe you're making your career an idol? It seems like everything rises and falls on what your boss thinks of you."

"You can't spend your life moping around, waiting for Mr. Right. What would it look like for you to live fully right now?"

"You often talk about wanting to do something big for God to make a difference, but are you being faithful today, even though it's mundane and not all that exciting?"

Ouch! In moments like these, pride can rear its ugly head. *How dare she tell me what to do or invade my personal life!* But wait. Isn't that what you asked her to do? Didn't you ask her to give you godly advice and feedback? Didn't you ask her to help you make wise decisions? Didn't you ask her to point you back to Jesus?

When your mentor touches a tender spot in your life, ask yourself, do I want to grow . . . or do I want to stay comfortable?

OF ELEPHANTS IN THE ROOM

"Conflict is inevitable, but combat is optional," Max Lucado writes.[1] I hate to admit it, but he's right. I wish I could tell you that if you find just the right mentor, you will get along like two peas in a pod. You'll never have a disagreement, always be on the same page, and every single conversation you have will be effortless and energizing.

If this is your experience, though, someone's pretending.

Either you or your mentor is not being honest. I pray your mentor will offer grace and love as she walks with you, but without her pointing you back to the truth of God as your guiding light, you will stumble around in the dark. It will do you no good for her to pat you on the back and tell you, "Do whatever your heart tells you" when she has concerns or red flags.

Just like you are taking the risk to be honest with her, so your mentor must commit to giving you honest feedback, even when it makes you squirm a bit. A good mentor will lovingly call you out on areas in your life that need to change: Blind spots you weren't aware of, things you've been ignoring, activities or behaviors you've been justifying, lies you've been believing. A mentor's role isn't to tell you what to do or force you in a certain direction, but to ask you thought-provoking questions and share godly wisdom from her life.

Will you listen? Or will you revert back to thinking you can figure out life on your own? Sometimes, you won't want to hear it. And sometimes, she may be off. That's why confrontation goes both ways. No one is perfect; your mentor will make mistakes. But when you feel hurt or misunderstood, it's up to you to go to her. Many of us don't know quite what to do with conflict or disagreements, so we resort to one of these not-so-healthy responses:

Run away! Maybe you avoid conflict like the chickenpox. When you disagree with something your mentor says or the way she challenged you, you start giving her the cold shoulder. You tell her you're "too busy" to meet right now, or come up with some other fairly lame excuse. But running away is a childish thing to do. Emotional maturity means sitting your tail in the chair across from her and talking it through.

Pretend everything's okay. *If I ignore it, it'll go away, right?* How easy it is to avoid the elephant in the room. As you sip coffee or walk through the park, you shift the conversation to anything and everything except what's irking you. My question to you is this: What's the point of having a mentor if you stop being authentic with her? Going through the motions of meeting doesn't guarantee you will grow and change. Honesty does.

Talk to someone else (or go on a Facebook rant). Whether you run away or just ignore the elephant, you'll inevitably be tempted to gab about your hurt feelings or irritation. That's because at your core, you long to work this issue out and find a solution. But talking with someone who isn't part of the problem or the solution will only spread gossip and further divide you and your mentor. And believe me, Satan will be laughing in glee.

Lash out and let her have it. If you're a confrontational person, maybe your biggest temptation is to lash out in anger. No time for pretense or niceties. You let your mentor know that she is out of line through a scathing email, a terse text, or the next time you meet: "I thought I could trust you to speak into my life with godly input, but you're just trying to manipulate me. And I won't have it!" Your emotions may be valid, but your attacking tone is not.

What's your gut reaction to conflict? I'm an elephant-keeper myself. I wish I was naturally good at resolving conflict, but I'm not. It's something I have to work at, and believe me, I've made a lot of mistakes! Whether the disagreement is with a roommate, boss, family member, or mentor, we each tend to have a default response. Take a moment to identify yours, and then consider, how well is it working for you? Is running away or lashing out getting you what you ultimately want—a stronger relationship with your mentor?

Perhaps we can discover a better way forward.

RESOLVING CONFLICT WELL

"I'm worried about you, Jayme . . . every time we meet, you talk about how crazy-busy life has been. Is there something you need to say no to?"

Doesn't she know that I don't have a choice in my schedule? I was irritated. *I have to work part-time. I have three young kids. And God just opened an amazing ministry opportunity for our family. I can't just waltz off for a spa day any time I want!*

Suzanne broke the silence of my brooding. "Jayme, I'm not saying this because I'm judging you. I've been praying about it for a while, and I'm really concerned. You can't keep up this pace for long. Your plate is way too overloaded.

"I've watched you ignore the warning signs and press on. But this stress is taking its toll on your health, even on your family. God's heart is for you to flourish and thrive, and that requires taking time to rest, to actually enjoy what He has given you. You are a limited human being, Jayme. You have a big heart, but you only have so much time and energy."

I was hurt. I was angry. I wanted to shut her down. But I knew she was right. God used my mentor that day to shine light on an area I'd been trying to justify and ignore—my schedule. I just wanted to be the exception . . . the wonder woman who was able to do it all.

Believe me, it was tough to admit that my life was bursting at the seams. That I didn't have it all together and was teetering at the edge of burnout. But by leaning into this confrontation, I became a much healthier person. When confronted by our mentor, we must remind ourselves that she loves us and wants what's best for us. She's not out to attack us.

Like it or not, conflict is a key part of every healthy relationship—from friendship to marriage to the workplace. And the good news is that disagreements and confrontation are key agents of change that God longs to use to shape you on the mentoring journey. It's new territory for many of us to realize that conflict is actually a catalyst for change and learning!

"Conflict is an opportunity to learn to love," psychologist Dr. Julie Gottman points out.[2] It's a novel idea, perhaps, but these challenges have the potential to create a deeper and more authentic relationship than ever, when we embrace them as an opportunity to grow.

There have certainly been times when my mentor has given me bad advice or unintentionally hurt me. Then what? The Bible encourages us to go to the person who has offended us and resolve the issue; see Matthew 18:15. Here are a few suggestions to keep in mind as you dive in.

Pray for clarity and a humble heart. Before you talk to your mentor, talk with God and search your heart. Write out at least five good qualities in your mentor that remind you why you want to resolve this conflict. Take time to consider, How did I play a role in this situation? What is it that I am ultimately upset about? How can I own my part? How can I approach my mentor with a desire to grow through this experience, not just prove my point?

Assume your mentor's intentions are good, even when you feel hurt and frustrated. This woman saw your potential. She agreed to walk with you and pour into your life in becoming the woman God created you to be. I doubt she woke up thinking, *Hmm . . . let me see how I can attack and hurt her when we meet today!* Far from it. Sure, she has her own weaknesses and imperfections, but don't forget her commitment to you.

Major on the majors, minor on the minors. You and your mentor will see differently on things, and that's actually a good thing! If you surround yourself with people who are all carbon copies of you, you won't be challenged to see God, yourself, and the world in a new way. However, it's easy to confuse principles (major tenets of the Christian faith) with preferences (minor differences in personality and lifestyle). So ask yourself, Is this a minor issue—a situation where I need to extend grace and agree to disagree? Or is this something worth bringing up?

Honestly express your feelings and concerns. Set aside a time to talk face-to-face, and don't beat around the bush. Share that something has been bugging you, and that your desire is to talk through it and find a solution. Describe the problem using "I" language: *I feel* _____ *when* _____. For example, "I feel frustrated when you jump in to answer before I finish talking." Express your core emotion. Did you feel misunderstood? Attacked? Afraid? Judged? Manipulated? Stay away from "You always/you never" generalizations.

Ask for your mentor's feedback and listen well. Emotions can easily cloud your judgment and transform your mentor into an enemy, which she's not! Don't get defensive or combative, and avoid dominating the conversation. Instead, be gracious and teachable. Invite her to think out loud with you, and welcome her feedback. Ask your mentor, Am I misconstruing the situation? What could I do differently in the future?

Work together to restore the relationship. This may include asking forgiveness, forgiving your mentor, and brainstorming together. For example, you might suggest, "I really value your input, but would you be willing to hold off until I get my thoughts out? Otherwise, my brain gets jumbled up and it's hard to listen." Keep in mind, this relationship and its formative impact in your life are far more important than your current disagreement.

DETOURS, DELAYS, AND DERAILMENTS

In my early twenties, I often took Amtrak home from New York City to Pennsylvania. Sometimes I was so exhausted that I fell asleep during the four-hour ride. This often meant waking up with drool on my face, feeling a bit disoriented. *Where am I? Why aren't we moving?* On a train, three different things can disrupt the journey:

A detour occurs when the engineer takes an alternate route due to repair work. In mentoring, detours may include confrontation and advice that's hard to accept. It's not where you saw the conversation going, but in the end, detours are good for us. Detours protect us from charging ahead on an unsafe track. Detours help us move forward in life with wisdom, if we're humble and open to learn.

A delay happens when the train must stop and wait its turn at a switching station. Here, the engineer needs to wait on train traffic before entering a new track in order to avoid a wreck. Hurt feelings, misunderstandings, and disagreements can bring mentoring to a screeching halt. Your relationship may feel shaky in the moment, but this is not a train wreck. A delay is temporary. With patience, honesty, and forgiveness, you and your mentor can get on a new track.

A derailment takes place when the train actually runs off its rails. Maybe you have a big blowup or you reach an impasse. Maybe there was some obstruction in front of you, but you ignored it. Derailments are often caused by "poor maintenance of tracks, collisions with other trains, improper switch assignment, overworked and tired train crews, improper removal of obstructions near railroad crossings, and excessive speed in poor weather conditions."[3]

Do you notice the common denominator here? **Derailments usually occur because of lack of communication**—pushing ahead ignorantly when you and your mentor really need to stop and talk. A simple detour or delay, if ignored, can lead to a relationship-threatening derailment. A derailment in mentoring leaves us wounded, discouraged, and defeated.

In some cases, even a derailment can be resolved and the relationship mended. If one train car derails just a few inches it can likely be repaired using rerailing frogs or just plain wood wedges along with the locomotive. The wheels can be realigned to enable the train to continue its journey safely. However, if the cars careen across the land at a hundred or more miles an hour or fall into a nearby gulley or river, the result can be deadly. When you ignore conflict, it can eventually sabotage—and potentially destroy—the mentoring relationship.

As you seek to resolve conflict with your mentor, how can you discern the difference between a detour, a delay, and a derailment—between a conflict to resolve and grow through, and a conflict that's a deal breaker? This is a complicated question to wrestle with. Every mentoring relationship is unique, but it's important to be honest about your concerns, early and often. Many a derailment can be prevented if you are proactive about resolving conflict.

Here are some warning signs that suggest you probably need to sit down and have a talk:

- If your mentor is talking behind your back and not maintaining confidentiality.
- If you find yourself guarded, on edge, and don't feel safe to be honest.
- If your mentor cuts you off, doesn't listen, and is constantly in "fix it" mode.
- If you find yourself tolerating her or coming up with excuses not to meet.
- If your mentor is not scripturally sound and is offering you ungodly advice.
- If you find yourself more worried about pleasing your mentor than God.
- If your mentor is using the relationship as an excuse to get her own needs met (pressuring you to dog sit, run errands, design her a logo, etc.).

I know this isn't a fun list to read. Nobody wants to face this kind of stuff—and I'm not saying it will happen to you. My hope, though, is to equip you so that no matter what lies ahead on your mentoring "track," you'll be confident and prepared to address it and resolve it.

Be encouraged! If you can learn to work through conflict face-to-face, you'll be miles ahead of your peers. Many of us hesitate to speak up, but learning to do so in a courteous and respectful manner will not only save time but will help us not stew over problems or become critical. That's what I want—to not waste time wallowing, but engage in productive dialogue.

EMBRACING THE STRUGGLE

The early church was no stranger to conflict! When Paul was transformed from one who persecuted Christians, imprisoning them and sometimes being involved in their deaths, to being a follower of Jesus himself, he was eager to join the rest of the disciples (see Acts 9).

The disciples weren't so sure. *Maybe it's all a trap. Isn't this the guy who's been throwing people in jail for believing in the Messiah?* I probably would have been pretty skeptical myself!

But not Barnabas. This guy saw the potential in Paul and "took him and brought him to the apostles" (Acts 9:27). Barnabas was Paul's first mentor. He played a critical role in shaping the character of Paul as a new believer and preparing him for a lifetime of ministry.

So just who was this Barnabas? Why did he take the risk on Paul? The Bible tells us Barnabas was "full of the Holy Spirit and faith" (Acts 11:24). Wherever he went, Barnabas brought encouragement, grace, and a renewed excitement about following Jesus. Barnabas "saw what the grace of God had done, he was glad and encouraged them all to remain true to the Lord with all their hearts" (Acts 11:23). *That* is the kind of mentor I pray God blesses you with!

Barnabas empowered Paul in becoming who God created him to be. They worked side by side for years in spreading the good news of the gospel. But even their relationship did not escape conflict. At one point, "They had such a sharp disagreement that they parted company" (Acts 15:39). Barnabas wanted to extend grace to a wayward disciple, inviting John Mark to rejoin them on their travels. "But Paul did not think it wise to take him, because he had deserted them in Pamphylia and had not continued with them in the work" (Acts 15:38).

Not the cloudless sky in the relationship we hope for. But in this imperfect world, relationships sometimes won't work out. And that's okay. The beautiful thing is that God continued to work in and through Paul, Barnabas, and Mark, even though they parted ways. Since you can't control your mentor's actions and responses, there may come a time when you need to part ways, too. Breakups are never fun—in dating or in mentoring —but sometimes, it's what we need to do in order to move forward. I have been part of mentoring relationships that ended because of value clashes, personality conflicts, and different understandings of mentoring. But even this doesn't have to be a crash-and-burn derailment.

When we're hurt, it's easy to lash out at our mentor or even seek to destroy her reputation. Yet Paul—the very one who eventually split with his mentor Barnabas—challenges us, "Don't hit back; discover beauty in everyone . . . Don't insist on getting even; that's not for you to do. 'I'll do the judging,' says God. 'I'll take care of it' " (Romans 12:17–19 MSG).

The way you end a mentoring relationship is just as important as how you begin. If at all possible, have a final face-to-face meeting. Be an adult. Don't just avoid her or stop returning her calls. When you meet, calmly explain your decision. Apologize for your part and try to understand her perspective. Thank her for investing in your life. Work toward forgiveness—it will set you free to begin to heal and trust again. God has a plan and a purpose, even in this.

Rather than letting the discomfort of conflict paralyze you, lean into it. "The desire for ease, comfort, and stress-free living is an indirect desire to remain an 'unseasoned,' immature Christian," Gary Thomas reflects. "Struggle makes us stronger; it builds us up and deepens our faith. But this result is achieved only when we face the struggle head-on, not when we run from it."[4] So don't run away. Don't throw in the towel and say, "I told you mentoring would never work." Maybe it *is* doing its work in your life right at this moment.

Welcome this struggle as a gift—a relational lab, so to speak. Conflict is one of those areas where your mentoring relationship is a safe place to try out new things, make mistakes, and build your relational skill set. Your spouse, boss, coworkers, and friends will thank you for it!

How can you embrace the challenges in your mentoring relationship as an opportunity to grow? No matter what conflict you face, I encourage you to consider, What am I learning—about myself? About relationships? How does God want to reveal Himself in the midst of this?

Let's connect authentically, forgive wholeheartedly, and love without regrets.

Respond

1. What is your gut reaction to conflict? Run away?
   Pretend everything's okay? Talk to someone else? Lash

out and let the person have it? Can you think of a time that you handled a conflict well? What did you do differently?

2. "Disagreements and confrontation are key agents of change that God longs to use to shape you on the mentoring journey." Do you agree? Have you ever found it to be true that God grew you through a conflict?

3. What character traits do you need to develop in order to navigate twists and turns in your mentoring relationship? How can you get through a detour? A delay? A derailment?

4. Where do you see yourself in the story of Barnabas and Paul? Has someone ever taken a chance on you?

5. "Don't throw in the towel and say, 'I told you mentoring would never work.' Maybe it is doing its work in your life right at this moment." How can you practically lean in to conflict this week and embrace struggle as a lab that builds your relational skill set?

9

Balance in a Crazy World

*Never is a woman so fulfilled as when
she chooses to underwhelm her schedule
so she can let God overwhelm her soul.*

LYSA TERKEURST

I've been soooo busy lately. It's like I'm sprinting on a tread-mill and it won't slow down. I feel the weight of anxiety just thinking about the millions of things I need to get done.

"Deadlines at my job. Working out. Grocery shopping. Cooking. Paying bills. My community group. Not to mention serving at church and trying to be intentional with friends.

"My life is insane, Jayme. I'm running at full-speed from 6 a.m. until 10 p.m. When I get home, I fall into bed like a zombie, dreading the fact that I have to get up and do it all over again."

"But do you?" I challenged her. "Do you really have to live

your life this way? After all, it's *your* life. No one is making you so crazy busy, are they?"

She thought for a moment, taking this new idea in. "I don't know . . . I feel like I have to. I look at the women around me and they seem to be juggling everything way better than me—and some of them are in grad school or have kids too. I feel like I don't measure up.

"When I say yes my schedule never looks crammed, but every day I'm frazzled trying to keep up. I run late. I get irritated and short with people. I never have enough time. So I grab an extra cup of coffee or two and try harder. I'm exhausted—but I can't say no!"

Her eyes welled up with tears. She was frustrated, worn out, and shackled by striving.

"I wonder what would happen if you did say no?" I asked. "If you stepped off that treadmill, even for just an afternoon?"

"Whenever I try to slow down," she said and sighed, "all I can think about is everything on my to-do list. Saturday, I slept in and chilled around the house, and I felt, well, really guilty.

"I hate that feeling, so I jump back in. I run faster. Get up earlier. Sometimes I wonder, though, the Bible talks about abundant life, but I feel stressed and empty . . . like I'm a big fat failure. God must be so disappointed in me.

"When you share about your relationship with God, well, it seems so real. So alive. It's like Jesus flows out of you and splashes on everyone you meet. I'm sure you have your busy days, but you're somehow able to stay centered and grounded, no matter what life throws at you.

"And me? To be honest, God is more of an idea I believe in—for heaven one day—than a person I know and follow today. As you talk, I'm intrigued. It makes me believe that there's more. I try to please God, as best as I know how, but there's some kind of disconnect."

Maybe you've been there. Running through your week at breakneck speed. You wish you could slow down, but you're not sure how. Your legs buckle underneath as you try to mount the treadmill one more day. It's slavery, this monster of *doing*. It lies to you every time.

Could it be the angst you feel is the truest compass back to the heart of Jesus?

ACKNOWLEDGING OUR LIMITS

As a kid, my favorite circus acts were the jugglers and the plate-spinning clown. I held my breath as the juggler kept multiple fire torches in the air, his hands a blur. One miscalculation, and he'd go up in flames. The clown equally amazed me, spinning half a dozen china plates on his head, fingers, nose, and toes! Miraculously, he kept those plates spinning every time . . . well, for the entire two minutes his show lasted.

But even clowns and jugglers can't go on forever. What makes us think we can?

And when did we buy into the idea of a one-woman show? Too often, I try to be the juggler, the acrobat, the lady shot out of the cannon, the trapeze artist, the elephant wrangler, *and* the popcorn and cotton candy seller, all wrapped up into one!

We don't want to miss out on God's will, or end up on the wrong path, so it's easy to say yes to everything! Before we know it, our sticky cotton-candy hands slip off the trapeze bar and we're free-falling. Thank God for a safety net!

I've crashed and burned a few times in my life. It's never fun. My spinning plates were teaching piano lessons, supporting my husband in running his business during the day and going to law school at night, teaching weekly Bible studies, blogging, mentoring women, praying my kids through college. Far too much for any one human being!

Jayme, what were you thinking? you ask. That's just the point—I wasn't. Not only was I not thinking, I wasn't sleeping. And junk food was my fuel.

I got the call that my dad had a blood infection, so I jumped in the car to make the twelve-hour drive to be with him in the hospital. Calling my mentor Linda while I was on the road, I poured out my heart, whining about how crazy busy my life was.

Linda listened and empathized, but she didn't stop there. She spoke truth into my life: "Jayme, you can't keep living at this pace. It'll ruin your health and take its toll on your family. Why not take your driving time to pray and ask God what you need to say no to?"

Ouch. I didn't want to accept her godly advice, but I knew she was right.

Nearly two-thirds of women describe their life as "too stressful," and that number jumps to 80 percent for women with children.[1] According to this study, women today are dissatisfied "with life's basic rhythms" and view rest as a luxury they don't have time for.

For many of us, our Achilles' heel is one short word: *Yes.* We say yes to everything, spreading ourselves too thin either to keep people happy or out of a legitimate desire to serve others. But as Lysa TerKeurst points out, "We must not confuse the command to love with the disease to please."[2] When we do, there's no energy left for what God is actually calling us to.

Wisdom is not just knowing when to push through, it's also knowing when to stop. No matter how hard we try, we can't do it all—work, family, friends, ministry, and the list goes on. You and I are limited human beings. Even the circus goes to sleep at night.

Stewarding our time and energy wisely starts with identifying what matters most. Not reacting to life or running about helter-skelter. But knowing who you are and what you're about.

What plates are you spinning? For just this moment, put them down. Relax. Breathe. None of us can run at 100 percent 24/7, and if we live in denial of this reality, we'll soon have a mess on our hands . . . and not just broken china.

UNPLUG, RECHARGE

We all have those little things in life that drive us bonkers. For me, it's when the dreaded words "10% of battery remaining" pop up on my iPhone. I am the queen of forgetting to plug my phone in at night. By mid-morning the next day, I realize the end is near.

Let me just finish this email, I tell myself. *Oh, and text that friend about lunch. And pay a bill. And return that missed call.* My fingers move at the speed of light, trying to escape the inevitable reality that my phone is dying. I hate to admit it, but too often, I squeeze out the last bit of juice and push my iPhone to the moment of black nothingness.

I can talk to my phone, I can set it out in the sunshine or next to my Mac, I can even plug the cord in at its base, but until I plug the other end of the charger in to an outlet, it's a no-go.

It's the same way with us and God. Huffing and puffing along on the treadmill of crazy-busyness, we'll eventually hit the spiritual red zone—that last 10 percent. Ultimately our faith will run out, and no amount of human effort or trying harder can revive it.

We need Jesus. He is our life source, our center in a chaotic world. Just like I need to plug in my iPhone each night to recharge, our spiritual vitality is dependent on daily saturating our heart and mind in His truth, His presence, His reality.

Just ask Martha. A woman of vision and faith, Martha treasured her relationship with Jesus. But Martha, like me, was a doer. When Jesus and His disciples were passing through her town, "Martha welcomed him and made him feel quite at home" (Luke 10:38 MSG).

Go Martha! Most likely, this wasn't a scheduled visit. Jesus showed up in Bethany, and Miss Hospitality said, "C'mon over!" Ever done that before? And then you realize your apartment is a mess, there's laundry to fold, and dinner isn't cooked? Talk about a panic attack!

That was Martha's feeling exactly. She quickly got pulled away from the conversation, preoccupied with the demands of the moment. Chop, cut, dice, boil . . . this gal didn't have the luxury of ordering takeout. We often judge Martha for being so busy, but seriously, do you blame her? If Jesus showed up at my house, I'd want to cook Him the best dinner I could!

In Jewish culture, Martha was doing everything right to honor her guests. She was responsible, hardworking, and hospitable.

As Martha broiled the lamb, she was broiling, too. *This is so unfair! How could Mary leave me all alone to cook for this group of hungry guys? I'd give anything to be hanging out with Jesus, too, but someone has to put food on the table!*

Finally, Martha couldn't hold it in anymore. She interrupted the conversation and dumped her truck on Jesus: "Don't you care that my sister has left me to do the work by myself? Tell her to help me!" (Luke 10:40). According to Jewish tradition, women were responsible for cleaning, cooking, and running the home. Mary's place was in the kitchen too!

I can't keep all these plates spinning, Jesus! Martha pleads. *Send me some backup!*

Jesus affirms Martha's good intent and desire to please Him. "I get it. You're freaking out. You want to honor Me by giving Me your very best," is His message to her. "But forget about the three-course dinner. I want to spend time with you! The best hospitality you can give is opening up your heart and making room in your life."

In all of her hard work, Martha missed the ultimate purpose of Jesus' visit. How often do you and I do that too? We forget the point of life! We overload our schedules with events, service opportunities, and appointments.

Before we know it, we've become human doings instead of human beings, as some say. I wonder, what kind of hospitality does Jesus receive in your life? Are you so busy planning your career and setting goals for your future that you neglect to just sit with Jesus? Sure, we all have work to get done every day—Martha had to cook dinner at some point—but we, and Martha, must realize that God doesn't ultimately want our work, He wants our hearts.

There will always be crazy-busy moments, days, maybe even weeks. But to build a sustainable and balanced life, we have to create (and fight for) rhythms of rest. The only way to recharge from the craziness and exhaustion we often feel is by unplugging and being with Jesus.

"He leads me beside the still waters. He restores my soul," David writes (Psalm 23:2–3 ESV). What are your still waters? When do you unplug? For some of us, it's setting our phones down. Taking a walk. Listening to worship music. Journaling. Taking a nap. Going for a run. Each of us has different rhythms, and there's no one "right" way to de-stress. But a key part of becoming a healthy adult is taking care of yourself.

Sabbath rest—whatever that looks like in your life—isn't just a nice idea. It's a command. Unplug from stress, from to-do lists, from worrying, from planning, from doing.

And instead plug in to God. Recharge your soul, mind, and body. Listen.

LIVING LOVED

How do I know when God is speaking to me? It's a question we all struggle with. As we join Mary and sit at Jesus' feet, how do we tell the difference between our own thoughts and the Holy Spirit speaking to our hearts?

Think about it this way. When John calls me from work, I hear his voice on the other end of the line: "Hi honey, how's your day?"

Instantly, I know who it is. John doesn't have to explain, "Jayme, this is your husband. You married me back in 1980—over thirty years ago. I'm six foot two, I have dark brown hair, and listen: I have a deep, calm voice. Remember? It's me."

That would be weird, wouldn't it?! And not romantic at all.

John doesn't have to give a long and formal introduction because I know him! At this point in our lives, we've been married longer than either of us was single. We've raised three children together; we've fought, cried, and prayed together; we've seen each other at our best and worst moments.

And over the years, I've developed this sixth sense. I know John's character. I often know what he's thinking. I can pretty accurately guess how he would respond in a given situation or the advice he would give me. I can even pick up on what he's feeling.

I know John because I am intimately involved in his life. I recognize his voice. It's the same way with God. We begin to recognize God's voice by getting to know Him personally through His Word. *What is His character? What is important to Him? How does He work in our world? What does His heart ache for? How does He feel toward us?*

"Cease striving," the Lord invites us, "and know that I am God" (Psalm 46:10 NASB). *Yada*, the Hebrew word for 'know,' describes an intimate, experiential knowing. In fact, it's the same word used in Genesis 4:1 (ESV) when "Adam knew Eve his wife, and she conceived." Nothing abstract there! Adam didn't just know facts about his wife, he knew every detail of her body.

"And this is eternal life," Jesus echoes, "that they know you the only true God, and Jesus Christ whom you have sent" (John 17:3 ESV). The Greek word used here, *ginóskó*, shares the same meaning: an intimate knowing, an experience that bears fruit.

God is eager for you and me to experience Him personally, not just believe the right theology. Do you really know God, or do you just know about Him? We discover the heart of Jesus by opening up God's Word each day, spending time soaking in its truth, and sitting in God's presence—not with a laundry list of requests, but an earnest desire to know Him. And that's where your mentor comes in.

For many of us, this is a far cry from our "quiet time" ritual of flipping through the Bible to read a verse or two. Duty and guilt can push us into a routine, for a short time at least, but empty rituals are of little value in getting to know God intimately.

I'm so grateful that it doesn't take a degree in theology to hear God's voice—in fact, childlike faith and an open heart are all we need. No more guilt, striving, or spiritual performance. No more "I have to read three chapters" or finding a verse to post online.

Just this: *God, give me a deep, passionate desire for You. I want to know You more.*

I challenge you to set aside all the rituals you may have accumulated over the years and try something new. Open up your Bible in search of a relationship. Get to know the person of Jesus Christ, and as His truth percolates down into your heart, you may just discover a new way of *being* fully yourself. In the words of Sarah Bessey:

> Living loved, we relax our expectations, our efforts, our strivings, our rules, our spine, our breath, our plans, our job descriptions and checklists; we step off the treadmill of the world and the treadmill of religious performance. We are not the authors of our redemption. No, God is at work, and his love for us is boundless and deep, wide and high, beyond all comprehension. He remains faithful.[3]

Hearing God is not just for the super spiritual—it's for you and me, now. Today. "Whether you turn to the right or to the left," God promises, "your ears will hear a voice behind you, saying, 'This is the way; walk in it' " (Isaiah 30:21).

Wow! I want that kind of guidance and closeness with God in my life!

God's deepest desire is for you and me to know and love Him with all of our heart, mind, soul, and strength. Really love Him with all that we are. Not like we love chocolate or working out. This kind of love changes us, from the inside out. As we soak up God's love for us, our hearts begin to shift. Our center is no longer doing or comparing. Our center is a God who loves, gives, forgives, redeems, and is with us. And that is a safe place to call home.

THE WOMEN YOU KNOW

I encourage you to incorporate rhythms of rest into your own life, and think beyond yourself too. Who do you spend time feeling energized and encouraged by? A woman who is balanced and centered, rather than chaotic and crazy.

Whether you run into her at the gym, at church, or at the grocery store, you walk away feeling more alive. You're drawn to her. She's not just making it, she's really living!

She may be busy, but when she sees you she doesn't brag about how much she has on her plate. Instead, she asks about you. She listens, really listens. Even if it's just in the cereal aisle or in the waiting line for the bathroom. Her life radiates passion, purpose, and hope.

She's authentic, too. Not perfect by any means, but she owns her weaknesses and past mistakes, and she's always learning and growing. Just talking with her makes you feel more comfortable being *you* . . . and it makes you want to grow, too.

Perhaps a few names come to mind of women like this. Jot them down in the margin.

The best place to start in connecting with a mentor is evaluating your current connections. Look for the women you want to become more like—in any area, but especially in this area of balance and tuning in to God.

Even as I'm writing these words, I'm breaking into a dance. I am confident that your mentor is just around the corner. Why? Because God is already in your future.

So let's start looking together!

Respond

꙳

1. "Our Achilles' heel is one little word: Yes. We say yes to everything, spreading ourselves too thin to keep people happy or out of a legitimate desire to serve others." Do you have a hard time saying no? What gets in the way of setting boundaries for yourself?

2. Reflect on your current commitments and pace of life for a moment. What plates are you spinning? What area do you need balance in? What limits do you need to acknowledge?

3. Who can you relate to more—Mary or Martha? Why? If Jesus stopped by your house and sat down at your kitchen table, what might He say to you? How can living loved set you free?

4. "To build a sustainable and balanced life, we have to

create (and fight for!) rhythms of rest." What do you need to say no to so you can tune in to God? How can you practically unplug, relax, recharge, and let God restore your soul on a day-to-day basis?

5. What women in your life do you admire and look up to? Pray about and evaluate your current connections as you begin to seek out a woman to mentor you.

Section Four

Living Authentically

10

Moving Forward

You are not what others think you are.
You are what God knows you are.

SHANNON L. ALDER

I can't shake the feeling that I'm never enough," she said with a sigh. "Not smart enough. Not mature enough. Not pretty enough, thin enough, or outgoing enough.

"I look at all my friends . . . and they seem to have their lives figured out. Jessica is getting her doctorate. Sarah started her own nonprofit. Natalie is traveling the world. Luci is married with two kids. Amy manages a team of fifty employees.

"And me? I'm not even sure what I want. Some days I wonder who I am . . . or if I'll ever amount to anything."

Not holding back, my friend spilled out her heart. "What the heck am I doing with my life, Jayme? I'm coming up on thirty this year . . . and what do I have to show for it?

"A college degree. A bunch of student loans. Several failed relationships. A few extra pounds, even. Sure, I have a few things on my resume, but nothing spectacular.

"When I was younger, I wanted to take the world on by force. You know, do something great for God. Like build wells in Africa or defend innocent victims in court. Help people in crisis or change the education system. I wanted to actually make a difference, but now I feel like I'm just making money and trying to pay bills.

"Is this what being an adult is? Because I don't like it. I want my old self back. The woman who dreamed . . . who believed anything was possible.

"These days, when I wake up, all I see is who I'm not. I feel like a big fat failure. No matter what I accomplish—even last month when I was nominated for Employee of the Week— there's this little voice inside of me that whispers, if they only knew who you really were, they would strike your name off that list in a heartbeat.

"I just feel so stuck. I know the Bible talks about who we are in Christ. I've heard it a thousand times." She rolled her eyes. "I know I shouldn't define myself just by what I do . . . but what I do still matters, right?

"It's like comparison has got a hold of me and won't let go. I can't even enjoy the good things God has given me. Can you help me find a way out?"

I reached across the table to reassure her. "I've been there, too. This monster of comparison will eat us alive if we let it. But who are you—at the core? Not where do you work or where do you live . . . those things can change in a heartbeat. But what makes you you?"

It's a tough question, but one worth exploring. How easy it is to get sucked into the busyness of the moment and go through life on autopilot. But sometimes something wakes us up on the inside and we're forced to consider who we really are, where we've come from, and what we're moving toward in life. This is an incredible gift.

So if you find yourself wrestling with some of these same questions, you're in a good place, my friend. A place of opportunity and discovery. Even if it doesn't feel that way.

DANCING DOWN THE YELLOW BRICK ROAD

"Show us what you're made of." From childhood sports to the competitive job market, performance is woven into the very fabric of our society. And the religious version is not all that different. "Do something big for God. Be a super-Christian."

Maybe your mom admonished you to be a "good little girl and make mommy proud." One way or another, you learned that who I am = what I do (or don't do) + what other people think of me. And if you're like me, you've been dancing ever since. We spend our days "running helter-skelter, always anxious and restless . . . never fully satisfied," Henri Nouwen reflects.[1] Doing, doing, doing. Yet beneath the veneer of doing good things, the cancer of striving can quickly set in.

It's easy to draw our sense of worth primarily from what we do, or don't do. Heather Holleman writes, "If you look back on your own life, you might see that you felt loved, important, and worthwhile if you were accomplishing something."[2] When we look to other people to tell us who we are, we're entering risky territory indeed. People are imperfect, sinful, and sometimes downright mean. If you've ever been to middle school, you probably know that firsthand. There will always be someone who disapproves of you. Maybe they feel threatened. Maybe they're jealous. Maybe they're just having a bad day.

When we mimic the dance steps of those around us . . . or dance harder to get an "attagirl," we often change who we are. Over time, doing deadens our souls to grace, and comparison enslaves us. We live in bondage to our productivity rating at work and the number of likes we get online. No matter how much we do, there's always one more thing left to prove.

Bit by bit, we begin to drift away from Jesus. We exile grace—it's too messy, and we're not that helpless anyway. We stop living in the reality of the gospel and instead try to manufacture our own good standing with God.

"For by grace you have been saved through faith," the apostle Paul writes. As if he anticipates our insatiable drive to perform, he goes on: "And this is not your own doing; it is the gift of God, not a result of works, so that no one may boast" (Ephesians 2:8–9 ESV).

By grace. We may talk about grace, we may have the words written in our journal, we may sing about grace on Sunday mornings, but it's little more than that. An abstract theological idea. We find our identity and worth in our accomplishments. We numb our insecurities and fears with the medication of comparison. But we can never do enough.

It's almost like we have an inkling that we are incomplete. Just like each of the characters in *The Wizard of Oz*: The Scarecrow wants a brain. The Tin Man longs for a heart. The Lion lacks courage . . . and Dorothy? Dorothy aches to find her way back home.

Which character do you identify with the most? Just like them, we are each flawed and incomplete. None of us are the perfect package. We are human, and our insecurities often arise from the stark reality of that humanness.

Yet while Dorothy and her friends hope to be rescued from their imperfectness and offered an easy solution, they instead must take a journey together, a journey that reveals their weaknesses, that stretches and grows them, and ultimately shapes in each of them what they lack. This is not unlike the journey of mentoring . . . a practical fleshing out of the transformation Jesus longs to work in each of our lives.

Getting through your identity crisis and tackling your insecurities is not a matter of trying to convince yourself that you are perfect, because none of us are. It's a matter of knowing that your imperfectness is not the final reality. Grace is. God's grace is undeserved and unexplainable. It's not based on what we do or don't do. It's based on God's unconditional love for us.

Too often, the church spends its time and energy helping us manage our sinful behaviors, but what our hearts long for is to grasp and live out of our true identity. An identity grounded in grace, not performance. Just like the troupe in the story looked to the wizard to make everything better, we often expect other people to tell us who we are. But what if who I am = chosen, treasured, accepted, valued, worthy of love and belonging, and enough? This is our forgotten identity. We are God's beloved children, and thus we have nothing to lose and nothing to prove.

This reality can free us to dance down the yellow brick road, not trying to dance like someone else, but free to be fully ourselves as we ask God to change and grow us with each step. To give us courage, a soft heart, and a wise mind. To show us the way home to our true selves.

IDENTITY EXPLORATION

Throughout your twenties and thirties, your identity will, I hope, flourish and grow in a million different ways. This is what psychologists call identity exploration—and there is no better time for it than right now. You may discover how much you love getting dressed up for work. You may discover the joy of traveling. You may uncover a hidden talent in art or writing or music. You may fall in love with learning and go back to school.

In fact, over the course of your life, you'll likely experience an untold number of changes and shifts, from relocations to loss of relationships, new opportunities to rejections and failures. How can you develop an identity that is strong enough to withstand change? An identity that grows and stretches to accommodate life's changes, rather than being destroyed by them?

After all, any of us can feel good about ourselves when life is neat and tidy and we have our dream job and the sun is shining and there is a cute guy on the horizon. But how can we stand firmly in who we know God created us to be, even in the middle of a rainstorm? Here's the secret: God didn't create you to be His little performer. He created you, first of all, to be loved.

This is the heartbeat of Jesus: Wild, reckless, unexplainable love. Love that knows no bounds. When you and I were spiritually dead and lifeless, God reached out with this love and chose us (Ephesians 2:4–8). I love the way Henri Nouwen puts flesh on these theological bones:

> We are the Beloved. We are intimately loved long before our parents, teachers, spouses, children, and friends loved or wounded us. That's the truth of our lives . . . The great

spiritual battle begins—and never ends—with the reclaiming of our chosenness. Long before any human being saw us, we are seen by God's loving eyes. Long before anyone heard us cry or laugh, we are heard by our God who is all ears for us. Long before any person spoke to us in this world, we are spoken to by the voice of eternal love. Our preciousness, uniqueness, and individuality are not given to us by those who meet us in clock-time—our brief chronological existence—but by the One who has chosen us with an everlasting love . . .[3]

The church throws around "who I am in Christ" statements haphazardly, and they quickly become cliché. It's not that we haven't heard them enough. It's that we've misapplied them. We've jumped to identity foreclosure. We've crafted cookie cutters and in essence said, "This is what a Christian looks like."

But God has created every single one of us unique. "For we are God's masterpiece," Paul reminds us. "He has created us anew in Christ Jesus, so that we can do the good things he planned for us long ago" (Ephesians 2:10 NLT). While our identity is shaped by our spiritual beliefs, that is not all that we are. Think about it this way.

If your identity is a pie, a lot of pieces will fill that pie, and this will likely change from season to season. You take pride at working hard, so a piece of that pie is your career. You flourish as you build a strong community, so another piece of the pie is your friends. Your family, your church . . . these are all pieces of the pie.

But your chosenness, being beloved by God . . . that's a different thing altogether. It's not a piece of the pie. It's the pie dish itself. It's the ceramic container that holds all the pieces of your identity steady and in place. You can share a piece of the pie, but the dish isn't going anywhere.

That's because while you are a lot of things, the truest thing about you is that you are God's beloved. This is a place you can rest and run to for shelter in the worst of life's rainstorms. No matter what happens in your life, even if you get laid off from your job or a relationship falls apart, you know who you are.

Sure, it will still hurt to lose a piece of the pie. You'll feel the emptiness. But it's not forever and it's not final. Because when God takes something away, it's usually because He can't wait to put another piece into your pie dish. Another piece of His dream for you.

Do you realize you have a pie plate? Or are you juggling slices of pie, trying to keep it all in the air? You don't have to. Soak it in for a moment: your chosenness. It is the crux of spiritual abundance, the secret to staying centered and grounded in your true identity, no matter what life brings.

INSECURITIES AND DREAM KILLERS

What triggers your insecurities? Beautiful women? Confident women? Smart women?

I know this may sound silly but ever since my teenage years, I've been insecure about what I'm wearing. I'm always walking back into the closet a couple of times and second-guessing the outfit I have on.

I can remember overhearing a few women's comments and snickers over another person's choice of clothes and thinking, "Wow. I think she looks fine. They must be talking about me behind my back in the same way." Never mind the media exploitation. The pressure from social media, television, movies, magazines, and more to have the perfect body shape and up-to-date clothes and accessories.

To be very authentic with you, I'm more insecure with the body I have to put in the clothes than I am about the clothes I'm wearing. If I leave this insecurity unchecked, I allow it to be used by the enemy to rob me of joy and kill the dreams God has placed in my heart. If I don't keep my focus on God's love for me and the unique way He created me, I can be derailed by lies about my appearance. I have to fight falling into that pit with everything I have.

So I make Psalm 139:13–14 (NLT) my morning confession. My confession of who I truly am: "You made all the delicate, inner parts of my body and knit me together in my mother's womb. Thank you for making me so wonderfully complex! Your workmanship is marvelous—how well I know it." Complex. Workmanship. Marvelous. This is who I am. And while I have a responsibility to take good care of the body God has given me, I will not tie my identity to the bathroom scale.

"We all have insecurities," Beth Moore writes. "They piggyback on the vulnerability inherent in our humanity. The question is whether or not our insecurities are substantial enough to hurt, limit, or even distract us from profound effectiveness or fulfillment of purpose. Are they cheating us of the powerful and abundant life Jesus flagrantly promised? . . . Are our insecurities snuffing the Spirit until our gifts . . . are largely unproductive or, at the very least, tentative?"[4]

Dream killers—we all have them. For me, it's my looks. This insecurity has the potential to keep me preoccupied all day, if I don't catch myself. When I live in fear of what other people will think of me, I easily second-guess myself. I hide, rather than stepping with God-confidence into each new day.

And I'm not the only one. Gideon was a hider too. Oppressed for seven years by the Midianite army, the Israelites were desperately trying to hang on. Waiting for a rescuer. Hiding. Since his family needed food, Gideon got creative. He turned their winepress (shaped much like a modern-day backyard pool) into a threshing floor. Imagine being so afraid that you drained all the water out of the pool and crept down to the bottom to work secretly.

Gideon was staying underground. Keeping things on the DL. But God found him there. The angel of the Lord greeted him, "The Lord is with you, mighty warrior" (Judges 6:12).

"You must be mistaken," Gideon responded. "I'm the youngest son in the weakest clan here in Manasseh. You must have the wrong guy."

The youngest. The weakest. Notice how Gideon defined himself by everything he wasn't.

Gideon had some questions for God, and I'm so glad he was brave enough to ask them: "If the Lord is with us, why has all this happened to us? Where are all his wonders that our ancestors told us about when they said, 'Did not the Lord bring us up out of Egypt?' But now the Lord has abandoned us and given us into the hand of Midian" (v.13). Do you feel the strong emotions? God has forgotten us. We will never amount to anything. We're a failure. We're not enough. Ever sung that tune?

The Lord responded to Gideon, not with a lengthy explanation, but plain and simple: "I will be with you" (v. 16). In other words, "Let those old labels go. I know your true potential in Me."

God did not see Gideon as he saw himself. God saw Gideon as He created him to be. His true identity was as a mighty warrior. But if Gideon had done what we often do, defining himself based on what people said, he might have come back with something like "wimpy farmer."

Do you see the difference? When God looks at us, He sees our potential. "The Lord does not look at the things people look at. People look at the outward appearance, but the Lord looks at the heart," Scripture reminds us (1 Samuel 16:7). There is no more surefire way to know who we truly are than by going back to the One who made us.

Gideon would go on to defeat an army of thirty-two thousand Midianite warriors with just three hundred men (you can read the full story in Judges 6–8). If you or I had told the hunkered down man in the winepress that he would go up against the Midianites with just three hundred soldiers, Gideon may have just had a heart attack. There's no way he could have dreamed that dream. It was God who wrote his story . . . and it is God who is writing our stories too.

What are your biggest insecurities . . . your dream killers? Who have you been comparing yourself to? How can you start rejoicing today in who God created you to be?

What if you started your day from a place of being loved? Being chosen. Being enough. Being a child of God. What if you planted your feet firmly here? Not a guilt trip to read your Bible or a halfhearted "be with me today" prayer. What if you stepped away from social media, set aside the mental list of things critical to get done today, and quieted your heart to listen for His voice? To hear the truth He is speaking over you. The truth of who you are.

Walking with a mentor can help you reclaim and live in this identity. It will make you a bold and powerful woman of God. It will free you to be yourself rather than trying to be like Jessica or Luci or anyone else. By connecting with a mentor, you can do the hard work now to discover who you are and what you want. You can explore your beliefs and what defines you. You can figure out where you came from and where you're going. You can stop reacting to life, and live it fully.

Respond

1. Which character from *The Wizard of Oz* do you identify with most? The Scarecrow? The Tin Man? The Lion? Dorothy? Why?

2. What makes up your identity? Draw out your own personal pie, with different sized pieces to represent the varying aspects of your life. How might you have jumped to identity foreclosure, rather than taking time to explore who God uniquely created you to be?

3. In what ways are you like Gideon? Take time to reflect on and list out your biggest insecurities. What does God want to say to you today about them?

4. Write out 1 Samuel 16:7 and underline the words that are powerful to you. If you want to go deeper, look up the Hebrew meaning of those words on www.biblehub.com or a similar site.

5. Take a moment to soak in the truth of Henri Nouwen's words when he says that we spend our days "running helter-skelter, always anxious and restless . . . never fully satisfied." How can you make this truth of your belovedness and chosenness a daily confession, not just a trite and clichéd statement?

11

In Search of Romeo

Don't live in a passive state of waiting,
but a chronic state of "this is the good life."
Go after your dreams. Don't wait for
permission or a partner or more money.

ANNIE F. DOWNS

This isn't the life I signed up for!" She sighed. "I'm supposed to be happily married with baby number two on the way by now. And here I sit . . . single and not even sure if I *want* to mingle."

She flung up her arms in frustration, and we both laughed, but her words were dripping with disappointment.

"My Facebook news feed is nothing but engagement pictures and darling little babies. They all look so *happy.* It's hard to not be jealous. I go to work, hit the gym, hang out with friends . . . and drive home to an empty apartment.

"I may not have a closet filled with bridesmaid dresses and

no wedding gown, but I'm getting close. I can fix just about any wedding crisis and paste a smile on, but inside, I'm screaming, 'What about me, God? When is it my turn?'"

Discontentment tore at her soul, a persistent, whiny voice that invaded many an otherwise happy moment with *if only you had a husband to share this with.*

"My parents' not-so-subtle pressure about wanting grand-kids only fuels my angst. Did I miss the boat? Am I undateable? Or too picky? Should I just marry the next guy who asks me out?

"As a little girl, I couldn't wait to finally grow up and meet *him*. I daydreamed about the first house we'd buy together, and how I'd decorate it with all the creativity in the world to stay within our newlywed budget. I imagined lazy Saturdays making breakfast together and the fun of surprising each other on Christmas morning.

"More than anything, I dreamed about sharing my life with someone . . . the taking-the-trash-out-grocery-shopping-making-a-budget kind of stuff. Just to be together. To walk through life side by side. But I'm beginning to lose hope.

"Life is a slap in my face: I am grown up. I'm paying my own bills, living independently, moved across the state to take this new job, trying to make friends, and still looking for *him*. I had no idea it was going to be this hard.

"Sometimes I feel lied to. I know logically that it's better to be single and lonely than stuck in a bad marriage, but it still hurts. All the Christian mumbo jumbo about waiting, trusting God, and letting Him write your love story. Maybe God lost His pen or something, because there's not much going on in my story."

It feels like a dead end: To trust God, to obey Him . . . and yet, to wake up each morning alone, facing the painful reality of unfulfilled dreams. The world urges us to abandon those old-fashioned morals and just have fun.

And the church's response? Well, you've read the books . . . perhaps you've thrown them across the room. Many of them full of clichés, formulas, and step-by-step processes promising a ring by spring.

Could there be a better way?

MORE THAN THE DREAM

When will my life begin? Rapunzel wonders. Snow White is saved by true love's kiss, Sleeping Beauty is rescued by the dashing Prince Phillip . . . and you and I? We dream on. According to a recent survey, only 20 percent of 18- to 29-year-olds are married, compared to 59 percent in the 1960s. So if you're wearing a wedding ring, you're in the vast minority.[1]

Somewhere between Disney movies and childhood daydreams, many of us have bought into the lie that "real" life starts when we walk down the aisle. That we're somehow less intelligent, less capable, less mature, *less than* as long as we are single. It's a myth that keeps us desperate and searching, looking to a relationship to affirm our worth and value, rather than starting each day from a place of being enough, chosen and valuable simply because we are God's daughters.

The dream can become all-consuming: find a good guy, get married, build a life together. Yet when we focus our attention solely on what we don't have, namely, Prince Charming, we fail to be present in where we are today and miss out on the sheer joy of simply being alive in this moment. We also bypass incredible opportunities to explore and develop our gifts and talents because we're more focused on who we are *with* rather than who we are *becoming*.

If you and I go through life searching for ultimate love and satisfaction in a guy, we may well end up gravely disappointed. And this is one key area in which discussions with a mentor will help us sort through. Because every man on the face of this planet is, well, quite human. Loving, committed, maybe; but also imperfect. Considering this, the apostle Paul wrote, "When you're unmarried, you're free to concentrate on simply pleasing the Master. Marriage involves you in all the nuts and bolts of domestic life and in wanting to please your spouse, leading to so many more demands on your attention" (1 Corinthians 7:32–33 MSG).

Simply put, marriage won't solve all your problems; it may just add to them. Now, I don't say this to devalue marriage in any way. I love my husband, John, and I am so incredibly grateful for him! However, in order to thrive exactly where God has each of us, we *must* dethrone the idol of a fairy-tale marriage. It just doesn't exist.

The world swings between the opposite extremes of "You are who you date" and "Guys are dumb and stupid and we'd be better off without them." We're told to take a side and join the club. *But wait.* Is singleness a wasteland of pent-up sexual energy to be endured and escaped from as soon as possible? Or is it something to be delighted in, enjoyed, and honored as valuable? Could singleness—just as much as marriage—be a gift?

Elisabeth Elliot speaks from experience here. In her twenties, she was single, married, and widowed. Reflecting on each of these seasons, she writes:

At age twenty-three, God gave me the gift of singleness. At age twenty-seven, the gift of marriage. At age twenty-nine, the gift of widowhood. I was not a wife anymore. I was a widow. Another assignment. Another gift. Don't imagine for a moment that was the thought that occurred to me. "Oh Lord" was probably all I could think, stunned as I was. One step at a time, over the years, as I sought to plumb the mystery of suffering (which cannot be plumbed), I began to see that there is a sense in which everything is a gift. Even my widowhood. I say I found peace. I do not say I was not lonely. I was—terribly. I do not say that I did not grieve. I did—most sorely. The peace of the sort the world cannot give comes, not by the removal of suffering, but in another way, through acceptance.[2]

I so appreciate her honesty. Loneliness? Grief? You bet it's there. Whether you're single or widowed or divorced, the ache of longing for what you've never had (or once had) is real and powerful. But somehow, Elisabeth honestly faced her emotions, rather than stuffing or running from them, while also refusing to let what she *didn't* have define her.

What about you? What defines your life? Another dateless Friday night . . . or the incredible people and opportunities right in front of you? Talking through and praying with a mentor is life-changing. If you open your eyes to see, rather than wishing you were somewhere else or with someone else. It reminds me of the words Elisabeth's husband, Jim Elliot, penned in his journal not long before his death: "Wherever you are, be all there! Live to the hilt every situation you believe to be the will of God."[3]

Now *that* is a far cry from waiting for life to begin with an engagement ring!

DARING TO LIVE FULLY TODAY

It's easy to feel forsaken when a guy you really like says, "You're amazing, but just not what I'm looking for." When the man you've given your heart to blindsides you with "I don't love you anymore." It's easy to feel sorry for ourselves on Friday night when Instagram is brimming with date night photos and cute couple collages, and then your married friend calls and asks you to babysit so she and her husband can go see a movie.

C'mon, seriously? We can so easily end up jaded or jealous. Resentful or raging. Desperate or disenchanted. How easy it is to spend our days just waiting in survival mode, for Mr. Right to come along and rescue us from the prison of our singleness.

But the truth cuts through it all, offering a better way:

"Don't be wishing you were someplace else or with someone else," Paul challenges us. "Where you are right now is God's place for you. Live and obey and love and believe right there. God, not your marital status, defines your life" (1 Corinthians 7:17 MSG). Blogger Amanda Bast wrestles honestly with this reality in her viral post, "26, Single, and Childless":

> Instead of relishing in the freedom, blessings and limitless possibilities that this stage of life offers me, I am left frozen, feeling like I'm not enough. Like what I've done doesn't really matter or that I've accomplished nothing. I'm an outcast. I'm defective. I'm panicked . . . [But] what if my ultimate goal has nothing to do with marriage or kids or a career? What if my aim was to love people well, and to fully embrace the gifts I've been given? Would that be enough? What if my life goal was to simply run the race, to be called

a good and faithful servant at the end of it all? Maybe that would mean marriage and children and a thriving career, but maybe it wouldn't. Is it ok if it doesn't?[4]

Christian culture often idolizes marriage, as if it were our sole purpose in life. Don't buy it. Don't buy this lie Satan longs to use to keep you in bondage, keep you passively waiting for a man to define you, rather than living fully today.

Every part of your story matters, and every part of your story God will use and redeem and transform. We've all made mistakes when it comes to guys. Guilt and shame can weigh us down and make us feel disqualified from being used by God. Moving forward with Jesus requires repentance and obedience, but Scripture is clear, "There is now no condemnation for those who are in Christ Jesus . . . you were washed, you were sanctified, you were justified in the name of the Lord Jesus Christ and by the Spirit of our God" (Romans 8:1; 1 Corinthians 6:11).

Jesus offers a fresh start, and in some mysterious way, He can get glory even out of your mistakes and failures. I challenge you to lay down the chains of regret and guilt and walk boldly in the truth, exploring the depths of God's love for you.

> [W]ith both feet planted firmly on love, you'll be able to take in with all followers of Jesus the extravagant dimensions of Christ's love. Reach out and experience the breadth! Test its length! Plumb the depths! Rise to the heights! Live full lives, full in the fullness of God. (Ephesians 3:17–19 MSG)

God created you on purpose, and that purpose isn't ultimately about your past mistakes, your relational status, or the jewelry on your hand. Cultivating your gifts and talents, growing into the woman He created you to be, building authentic community, and making a difference in your world to glorify God . . . that's living fully.

Contentment is trusting God with the future—with your dreams and desires and what you don't have—but it's also being fully engaged and present right where you are as you read these words. It's cultivating "a chronic state of 'this is the good life,'" as Annie Downs puts it.[5]

If you're a sweet tea lover like me, you've probably seen the iconic Nestea plunge commercial. (If not, Google it!) The storyline may vary a bit, but the main character is always in a similar predicament: driving through the sweltering desert, exhausted from moving into a new apartment . . . you get the idea. Pop open a bottle of Nestea iced tea, and after one gulp, the guy or gal falls back into a crystal blue refreshing pool that appears out of thin air. *Ahhh!*

Do you and I trust God enough to fall into His arms with the same abandonment? To fully enjoy the *today* He has given us? Go ahead. Drink up His love for you—it's even better than the best sweet tea!

KINGDOM WOMEN

From her first recon mission to save Moses's life to her influential role as a prophetess and leader, Miriam was on the front lines of God's work bringing the Israelites out of slavery (see Exodus 2—Numbers 20:1). Her life was defined by obedience, faith, and a willingness to step out without knowing what the future would bring. Miriam didn't cling to certainty. She clung to the promises of God. Though she was far from perfect, her wisdom, love, and diligence impacted an entire generation.

And the Bible gives no mention of her marital status. Scholars agree that she was most likely single in a culture where marriage and child-rearing defined womanhood. Yet Miriam didn't live in a passive state of waiting. She stepped out in obedience, letting God, not her marital status, shape her path.

Rebekah's life wasn't all that glamorous (see Genesis 24). After a long day of work, she went to the well with one purpose in mind—to get water. But when she was approached by an older man asking for a drink, she didn't hesitate. Cooking dinner and the million other tasks on her to-do list could wait. Rebekah chose to be present and engaged in the moment by serving Eliezer, and she went above and beyond to also offer to draw water for all his camels (see Genesis 24:45–56). Scholars estimate that her clay pot may have weighed forty pounds or more when it was filled, and that watering the camels may have taken three to five hours! Whew! Talk about a determined, gutsy woman!

Little did Rebekah know that Eliezer had prayed just hours before to meet her. And never in a million years could she have dreamed that she would leave her family, travel to a foreign land, marry a man she'd never met, give birth to twin sons, and be in the lineage of the Messiah.

Was it one kind act that changed Rebekah's life? No, it was a thousand moments. Rebekah's loving and caring posture that evening at the well flowed out of *who* she was as a woman . . . out of character that had been developed day after day, year after year as she plodded down the dirt path to draw water.

Miriam and Rebekah . . . two women who obeyed God right where they were . . . yet their life journeys are unique. As are ours. That's because for those of us who know God and follow Jesus, the ultimate goal is not marriage but investing in God's kingdom.

For some of us, like Rebekah, God brings a husband to walk through life with and serve together. For others, like Miriam, God uses us in powerful, culture-shaping ways through our singleness. One role is not superior, nor the other inferior. It's not like Rebekah did the "right" thing and Miriam made a mistake.

Each of our stories is written by the hand of our loving God. We all have dreams, and there are no guarantees. But I can promise you this. If you step out in bold faith and dare to live fully right where you are, you will not miss out on one second of what God has for you.

God calls us to be kingdom women. Women who live differently—who break the molds of feminism and fairy tales and start afresh. Women who neither build our lives around marriage nor abandon it either.

Women who honor, not degrade, men, but also who don't define ourselves by them.

Women who value both singleness and marriage as unique opportunities to love and be loved within the body of Christ.

Women who dive headfirst into each new day with God-confidence and a desire to change our world . . . right where we are.

Before you turn the page, take a moment to reflect on your life. Have you allowed yourself to be defined by your relational status? Ask God to open your eyes to the dreams He has for you. What are you passionate about? What makes your heart beat faster? What would you do if you didn't have to work and could do anything with your time? Write it down—this may well be a clue to your calling.

My prayer for you, dear friend, is that you will boldly pursue what God has put in your heart, rather than holding your breath just to get married.

Respond

1. "Whether you're single or widowed or divorced, the ache of longing for what you've never had (or once had) is real and powerful." What is the ache you feel?

2. Take a moment to reread Amanda Bast's "26, Single, and Childless" quote. What do you most identify with in Amanda's honest wrestling here? How can you fight the tendency to let what you don't have define your life?

3. Reflect on the words of 1 Corinthians 7:17. In what ways do you struggle with feeling less than and discontent because of your relationship status? What might it look like for you to live fully right where you are?

4. "God created you on purpose, and that purpose isn't ultimately about your past mistakes, your relational status, or the jewelry on your hand." What have you allowed to become your purpose in life—marriage, kids, something else? How would you like that to change?

5. What impresses you the most about Miriam's life? Rebekah's life? What step can you take today to become more of a kingdom woman rather than a damsel in distress, waiting to be rescued by a man?

12

Getting Unstuck

Growth is painful. Change is painful.
But nothing is as painful as staying stuck
somewhere you don't belong.

MANDY HALE

*I*t's so easy to go through life on cruise control. Work. Gym. Eat. Sleep. Repeat. I can go a few weeks without really stopping to think! That's why I wanted to meet you at the park today. Just to do something different."

The sun shining and the flowers in full bloom, it was a perfect spring day to soak up the beauty of God's creation (and start working on our summer tans too).

"Don't get me wrong, life's not *bad* right now," she continued. "I just wonder sometimes. As I was driving over here, a song came on that's *so* where I am right now."

She pulled the lyrics up on her phone, which included "climbing aimlessly over these hills . . ."[1]

"On the outside, I may look happy and put together, but

inside I feel so stuck—anxious, lonely, and searching for something more.

"I have to admit, I can be an adventure junkie sometimes. I love intensity. Traveling. Seeing new places. Experiencing life in a different way. So do I just need to settle down and change my expectations? Or is this angst I'm feeling really legit?

"I want to live intentionally. To really follow God. But so often, I think I react to life, rather than making daily decisions about what I want to move toward.

"Lately, it doesn't feel like I'm moving at all—just going through a routine that becomes less satisfying and more meaningless each day. I know routine and schedule are a part of being grown-up, but surely, there has to be something more.

"The funny thing is, I'm not even sure what's keeping me in this rut. Is it my job? Is it my boyfriend? Is it my friends? Is it *me*?

"I really need your wisdom here, Jayme. Maybe I have blind spots I don't recognize."

As my friend and I strolled through the park that day, taking in the hyacinths and forsythias and Bradford pear trees, she shared with me the new growth she ached for in her life.

This year, her spring cleaning wouldn't begin with tidying up her apartment, but de-cluttering her heart. Perhaps you can relate. Stuck in a rut. Trying to ignore the clutter in your life. What would it look like to find a fresh start? To break out of fear and regret and live fully?

THE STUFF WE CLING TO

I'm sentimental by nature, so I hold on to everything. Birthday cards. The kids' trophies. Clothes that went out of fashion five years ago. Wedding invitations. You get the idea.

There's nothing like packing to reveal just how much clutter has piled up. I hate to admit it, but with each of our moves, I inevitably find some boxes from the previous move, five or ten years ago, that were never unpacked.

The first time I took a load of stuff to Goodwill, I was incredibly anxious, convinced if I gave away that extra curling iron the one I kept would go up in smoke and then what would I do? *What if I decide next week that I really like that pair of boots? And that picture—what if it fits in our new house perfectly?*

Amazingly, though, my curling iron didn't short-circuit when I got home. And I didn't miss my scuffed-up leather boots. What I did feel, though, was incredibly free. No more stress about finding places to hide my clutter!

Life is not all that different. How easy it is for us to hold on to people, positions, places, or possessions that bog us down— that fill up space in our lives and distract us from our true purpose as kingdom women who follow Christ.

When you and I cling too tightly to anything or anyone, it doesn't end pretty. You may keep dating a nominal guy just so you don't have to face the pain of being alone.

You may stay in a job you should have left months ago for fear of the unknown.

You may feel guilted into staying in a ministry position when God is calling you elsewhere, just because they need help.

You may be paralyzed by the fear of making the same mistakes your parents did, so you don't get married at all.

You may keep hanging out with friends who push you to do things you aren't comfortable with for fear of having no social life.

You may cling to a destructive habit, even though you hate yourself for it, because it numbs the pain in the moment.

You'll know you're stuck when you keep going back to someone, something, or someplace that isn't good for you . . . something you need to let go of. You may not even know exactly *why* you do it, you just feel the pull. Author Ellery Sadler reminds us:

Friends walk away. Boyfriends leave. Pets die. Careers end. Families change. You can either be left with fingers stiff and sore from gripping so tightly, and a heart aching with the pain of treasures ripped away, or you can open your hand and let them go. Of course, some friendships, careers and relationships are worth fighting for with every breath in your body. But not everything is. Sometimes you need to open your fingers, hold out your hand and let it go. Learning to hold loosely is the key to living life well.[2]

If you live long enough, you'll experience loss. You'll get hurt. Things won't go as you expected. In those moments, if we cling on to people, places, and stuff with a death grip, our life will turn to quicksand. If we dare to let go, life will still hurt sometimes. But it won't pummel us. It won't destroy us. Instead, it will shape and develop us into beautiful women.

Uncovering the root of where you're stuck and why you're stuck is part of the mentoring journey. As you get connected with a mentor, I encourage you to ask her, What areas do you see in my life that I need to grow in? It takes a lot of humility to accept difficult feedback, but like my friend pointed out in the park that day, we all have blind spots. And those blind spots can lead us to dead ends faster than we imagine!

Getting unstuck isn't a onetime thing, either. It's a daily practice. Satan will always be setting a snare. If he can't keep you stuck in a relationship, he'll throw you the curveball of worrying about finances. If he can't paralyze you with guilt, he'll come at you with jealousy.

Anything to keep your eyes off the goal of becoming the woman God created you to be.

THE OTHER SIDE OF FEAR

A friend of mine calls these stuck places "muddy fields" along the journey of life. I love that. Regardless of your exact situation, I bet we have one thing in common: *fear.*

Did you know that fear is actually critically important? It's our internal "warning signal" when we don't feel safe, prompting us to make necessary changes. For many of us, anxiety echoes back to our history. We fear because we have been hurt, betrayed, abandoned, and the scabbed-over wounds are still tender.

Fear paralyzes us and keeps us stuck. Fear makes us hold on to stuff rather than holding on to God. Fear tells us to play it safe, rather than stepping out and taking appropriate risks to pursue the dream God has put in our heart. Fears about our future can be particularly crippling because our minds imagine every possible thing that could go wrong, forgetting God's presence and provision in every moment. But just the opposite is true!

Whatever is in your future—whatever joys or heartaches, celebrations or losses—this one thing I do know: God will meet you there, just as He longs to meet you in this moment.

His grace, faithfulness, and peace are there for the taking.

Anchoring our hearts in the reality of who God is *for* us and *with* us changes everything. As we learn to face our anxieties and bring them into the light of God's truth, we can step forward with wisdom and discover a new rhythm of life.

In the words of the psalmist, "Therefore we will not fear, though the earth give way and the mountains fall into the heart of the sea, though its waters roar and foam and the mountains quake with their surging" (Psalm 46:2–3).

Fearless at the cliff-edge of doom. How is that possible? Because we marinate our hearts in the unshakable reality that "God, your God, is striding ahead of you. He's right there with you. He won't let you down; he won't leave you" (Deuteronomy 31:6 MSG).

The world says, "Just do it. Follow your heart. Stop over-thinking this!" That's inspirational, sure, but it can lead us astray. We need godly wisdom to discern the movement of God in the midst of well-meaning advice from friends, our own passing whims, and cultural scripts that dictate what we *should* do. We need the input of a mentor.

I used to think that the other side of fear was recklessness. "Let go and let God," as the adage goes . . . whatever that looks like. Casting yourself over the edge mindlessly, without a thought to what comes next. But I've come to realize that true fearlessness is rooted in just the opposite: our souls' fresh awareness of God's presence. We are best equipped to make God-honoring decisions when we start from a place of knowing we are loved. We are secure. We are held. We are imperfect. We are beloved. We are worthy. We are redeemed. We are enough.

From this vantage point, we're not compelled to do CPR on a friendship or dating relationship we should have left months ago. There's no need to stay with a boyfriend just to avoid being alone. We can say no to a date, and we can say yes. We can turn down a job offer or seek one out. Both with confidence. Our actions are propelled by prayerful consideration and godly advice, not fear and skittishness.

"Courage doesn't mean you don't get afraid. Courage means you don't let fear stop you," Christian surfer Bethany Hamilton writes.[3] After losing her left arm in a shark attack, Bethany got back on her board, pushed through discouragement and depression to learn how to surf again, and now competes on an international level.

Getting unstuck is possible. Whether it's a dead-end relationship. A job that is sucking your life away. An addiction. Bitterness. Guilt. God longs to lead you out of bondage, to help you get back on your board and surf. But it won't happen in isolation.

Living fully starts with giving voice to your fears and questions in a safe place. Write them down. Tell someone you trust. Bring them to God. As Stasi Eldredge writes: "The places where we still fear are simply the places we have yet to fully receive God's love . . . It is an exchange of fear for desire. It is an exchange of death for life . . . God does not want you to live in fear. And he does want you to live."[4]

What's on the other side of fear? God—present, active, and intimately involved in our stories. You and me—courageous, bold, confident, free. Free from the endless "what-ifs" that zap our energy. Confident in who God has created us each to be. Bold to take risks and step out in obedience to God's leading with intentionality and purpose. And courageous to see that while our fears are real, they are not final.

A DREAMER WHO DIDN'T GIVE UP

Getting unstuck isn't just about a passive state of trusting God, it's also about intentional action. Consider the Old Testament story of Joseph. God gave this young man a dream, but the dream turned deadly when Joseph's brothers threatened to kill him, then sold him into slavery.

Handcuffed and stumbling across the desert, I can't imagine the fear and loneliness this guy felt. If I were Joseph, I might have easily stumbled into the mire of self-pity. I would have taken on the labels of "victim" and "abandoned." I would have stopped dreaming.

But Joseph didn't. Sure, he was afraid. He was lonely. He was heartbroken. But he didn't stay stuck in those emotions. Even as he grieved the loss of his family, Joseph worked hard as a servant for one of Pharaoh's officials. While Joseph didn't understand the "how" or "when" of God's promises, he chose to believe God was still at work.

And he was right! The Bible tells us, "When his master saw that the Lord was with him and that the Lord gave him success in everything he did, Joseph found favor in his eyes and became his attendant" (Genesis 39:3–4).

Joseph refused to stay stuck in bitterness, so the devil threw another hook his way—a beautiful woman. But Joseph saw past the pleasure of the moment to realize what the temptation was really about. He told her, "My master has withheld nothing from me except you, because you are his wife. How then could I do such a wicked thing and sin against God?" (v. 9).

Falsely accused by Potiphar's wife of attempted rape, Joseph was punished—not rewarded—for making the right choice. He ended up in jail. As if it couldn't get any worse, his brothers turned on him, he was sold into slavery, and now he's unjustly thrown into prison!

"God was still with Joseph . . . The head jailer put Joseph in charge of all the prisoners—he ended up managing the whole operation" (vv. 22–23 MSG). Though he was trapped in a jail cell, ironically, Joseph wasn't stuck. Rather than shaking his fist at God or passively trusting and waiting to be rescued, Joseph took intentional action to do good where he was.

He dared to believe that God's purpose for his life started here and now, even if it included mopping floors and managing prisoners. After thirteen years as a slave, Joseph is called on to interpret the pharaoh's dreams. In one day, he moves from jail to the palace, where God used him to save the people of Egypt, and his family, from famine.

What's your jail cell? We all have one, and if we let it, that circumstance, loss, or personal struggle will keep us living as a victim. For some of us, it may be past abuse, a dysfunctional family, crippling anxiety, difficulty trusting people, or something else. I've had my own share of jail cells over the years, but one of my toughest is needing other people's approval.

Some days, when I feel really stuck, I turn to this simple and well-known prayer: "God, grant me the serenity to accept the things I cannot change, the courage to change the things I can, and the wisdom to know the difference." We could easily rewrite the last phrase as, "and a mentor to help me know the difference." There's nothing like a mentor to help you get unstuck from the wrong thing and stick to God's promises and God's truth.

Some things in life we simply cannot change (even though we tend to freak out and fix and control). For Joseph, it was getting sold into slavery, being hit on by his boss's wife, and ending up in jail. For you and me, maybe it's an annoying boss, a family member who isn't following God, or a relationship that seems broken beyond repair. In situations we can't change, it's not just about coping or surviving. It's about finding God right in the middle of it; God, who wants to change and shape us and reveal Himself to us.

In other areas, we need to take intentional action, just like Joseph worked hard as a slave rather than becoming bitter, ran from temptation rather than compromising his values, and chose to forgive his brothers after all of the ways they had hurt him. For you and me, maybe it's the decision to move out. To take a new job. To break up. To forgive. To trust again. And that's where we need courage to take action, even when it's not comfortable, popular, or easy.

FRESH CEMENT

Ever noticed cracks in the sidewalk? The oak trees lining our neighborhood have left the pavement uneven and fragmented. Roots grow large, breaking the cement apart bit by bit. The pathway buckles up. And over time, weeds start to grow, struggling for life in those crevices.

When I go out to walk our dog Rascal, I see those cracks, and I remember. I remember summer night strolls with John and our three young kids. I remember running in the early morning light and counting those crevices, just to distract myself from the stitch in my side.

We can reminisce all we want, but one thing we can't do is reshape the cement. It's been hardened for decades. Just like our past. Our parents' decisions and mistakes and perhaps our own as well. Life's experiences shape us, affect us deeply. Faith cracks. Hope is splintered through. The gnarly roots of fear pierce through our dreams.

But the fresh sidewalk, the one that's being poured in the new subdivision next to ours, can be shaped into anything you desire while it's curing. You can leave your footprint or write a special message. Best of all, there are no cracks. It's smooth and wet and pliable. Just like the future we're creating each day. By our decisions. By our actions. By our faith.

We can't change the past any more than we can smooth over those cracks in the sidewalk. But our God is *I AM*. Not I Was or I Wasn't. I Will or I May Be. He is in the present—in the wet cement of our lives—eager to mold and shape us, mature and grow us.

"Do not dwell on the past," God admonishes the children of Israel (and us!). "See, I am doing a new thing! Now it springs up; do you not perceive it? I am making a way in the wilderness and streams in the wasteland" (Isaiah 43:18–19).

Following Jesus isn't a self-improvement project. He simply says, Come. Come exactly as you are . . . cracks, mistakes, messiness. Bring Me those fears that keep your heart in bondage. Fear of making the wrong choice. Fear of failure. Fear of missing out. Fear of being alone. Bring your anxieties into the light of My presence and safe community. I will meet you there. I will heal and transform you. I will shape your fresh cement into exactly the future I have for you.

What's holding you back?

Where are you stuck?

What do you want to change?

Bring Jesus your fear. Talk with your mentor. You'll begin to move from stuck to unstoppable.

Respond

1. Being stuck = "when you keep going back to someone, something, or someplace that isn't good for you." Where are you stuck? What can you do today to begin to get unstuck?

2. Consider and write out your biggest fears. Then, next to each one write a promise from the Bible about who God is *for* you and *with* you. How can you anchor your heart in the reality today that though your fears are real, they are not final?

3. Reflect on Stasi Eldredge's words on page 158. Underline the key words or phrases that stick out to you. How can you marinate your heart in God's love today to disarm your fears? Perhaps journal a prayer, or talk to God, or sit and soak up the truth of Psalm 46.

4. What's your jail cell—a circumstance, loss, or personal struggle that keeps you living as a victim? Do you ever wonder if God has forgotten you? How can you be

encouraged by seeing the end of Joseph's story, even though you can't see the end of yours?

5. Are there any intentional actions you need to take to get unstuck? If so, where can you start today? Who can you turn to for help and support (a friend, counselor, mentor, family member, etc.)?

Section Five

Pass It On

Pass It On

God has given us two hands—one to receive with and the other to give with. We are not cisterns made for hoarding; we are channels made for sharing.

BILLY GRAHAM

I want to give back. I don't just want to be a sponge—soaking up, learning, and growing myself. But I also don't want to jump into something too quickly, you know?"

My friend and I had been meeting for over a year. We'd wrestled through hearing God's voice, making career decisions, navigating the dating world, confronting personal insecurities, discovering her unique calling. You name it—we'd talked about it.

"I still have a lot to learn, so I hope we can keep meeting. But I feel like I'm finally in a better place with God and relationships and life, and I definitely want to pass it on. I wish I had someone like you in my life back when I was fourteen or sixteen.

"Those were some rough years," she reminisced. "Endless zits. Boy drama. I felt so weird and confused. I had so many questions and I didn't really have anyone safe to talk to. Maybe God can use me to encourage a girl who's feeling that way, too."

I'd been waiting and praying for the day when we would have this very conversation!

"You are spot-on," I assured her. "Mentoring is never just about us. It's about God working *in* us to prepare us for what He wants to do *through* us. And you don't have to be an expert or have gray hair to mentor someone else. It's about seeing the potential in another woman and walking with her in becoming who God created her to be. You can do that now!"

"I need to remind myself of that," she admitted. "As soon as I start thinking and praying about mentoring someone, a million insecurities pop up. All those lies of *not being enough* and *not having anything to offer* creep back in.

"And how do I know where God is leading me? I'm excited about the possibility of investing in other girls' lives like you have been so intentional with me, but where do I start?"

"I love how you want to proceed with wisdom. That is evidence you are growing!" I pointed out. "The reality is, God is already at work in a lot of those places you mentioned. But just because there's a need doesn't necessarily mean you are responsible to meet it. Let's really dig deep into what God is calling you to specifically, considering your passions and gifts."

My heart beat faster as we brainstormed and prayed together. A few weeks later, she excitedly shared that she'd signed up to coach girls' basketball for an urban rec league.

"These girls on the team—they don't have anyone who believes in them. I'm so excited to build their confidence in basketball, get to know their stories, and invest in them individually. They have so much potential . . . They just don't see it yet!"

What about you? If you're like me, I enjoy watching sports but I'm not the best one to coach. What's beautiful is that God uses our unique personalities and interests to connect us with other people. So don't force yourself to do something you hate. Go where your heart beats faster.

MENTORS IN DISGUISE

Long before I ever knew what mentoring was, I was being mentored. I'll never forget riding along in the Ford Pinto with my mom, singing at the top of our lungs on our way to pick up kids who needed a ride to church. Mom modeled for me practical ways to help and serve others, and we had a lot of fun doing it. Granted, Mom and I had our share of disagreements, particularly when I was a teenager! But Mom taught me to love, to dream, to never stop learning and growing.

My Grandma Fannie was the hardest-working woman I've ever met and she had a joy about her that was contagious. It was only as I got older that I began to understand the challenges in her life—how she lost her second baby to spina bifida, her unexpected divorce, her faithfulness working in factories for over thirty years. Grandma modeled for me how to find joy in the small things. Her life wasn't glamorous, but it was meaningful. She refused to allow sorrow and pain to make her jaded or bitter.

My high school drama director, Priscilla, wasn't afraid to challenge me. She pushed me to get out of my routine way of thinking and doing and become more confident being in front of people. When I had the role of Nancy in *Oliver,* she refused to let me slide by with mediocre acting and made me learn Cockney English for all my lines. I was irritated in the moment, but now, as I look back, I'm forever grateful. Priscilla believed in me when I didn't believe in myself. She wouldn't let me give up even when I wanted to. Week in and week out, Priscilla continued to encourage me and tell me I had potential.

Each of these incredible women has passed on, but their investment lives on through me. I love and give because of my mom. I fight for joy because of my grandma. And I refuse to give up because of Priscilla. These are just three of many women who have shaped who I am today.

Who has poured into your life? It may not have been called "mentoring" and you may not have had official meetings—but who have your role models been? Consider the people who took an interest in you, saw your potential, and never gave up on you.

Maybe it was your mom, maybe it wasn't. Maybe it was your teacher, your aunt, your coach, your neighbor, your Girl Scout director, your camp counselor, or your Bible study leader.

This woman may have been in your life for a short period of time or most of your childhood. You may have seen her several times a week or once a year. She may have been a follower of Jesus or held to some other faith. Regardless, though, without her, you wouldn't fully be the woman you are today, because this is how we grow—through relationships.

As Mother Teresa pointed out: "We have been created for greater things, not just to be a number in the world, not just to go for diplomas and degrees, this work and that work. We have been created in order to love and to be loved."[1]

Why not take a moment to thank God for bringing these women into your life to shape and grow you, even before you knew what mentoring was all about? Perhaps jot their names in the margin and consider their specific impact—the mark they left on you. How might God want you to hand down their investment? Will you hoard it—or will you pass it on?

RELAY RACES AND RUNNING TOGETHER

I've always wanted to be a long-distance runner, but in reality I'm slower than molasses, as my PE teacher would say. One event I'm fairly decent at, though, is relay races. As a relay runner, you go all out—you run your lap on the track with every ounce of energy you have—but when you come around the final curve and it's your turn to pass off the baton, you'd better slow down just a bit. "Everything is won or lost in the exchange zone!" our teacher often reminded us. Passing the baton is an art, really. Try to pass it off too soon, and the judges may disqualify you. Toss it to the next runner sloppily, and she may fumble and drop it. Hold on to your baton for too long, though, and your team will certainly lose ground.

Despite its challenges, my favorite part was always passing the baton to the next runner. For that moment, I felt important . . . connected . . . part of something bigger than myself. I was . . . and you are, too. After all, this isn't a one-woman race. A relay isn't about filling up the trophy case on your own. The only way to get across the finish line is together.

So where are you on the track today?

Have you mistaken this life for a marathon? Are you trying to run a relay race solo? It's a myth that you can create yourself and figure out life completely on your own. Your energy will eventually run out. You'll limp along, out of breath and with a stitch in your side. You may be able to survive, but you can't thrive running solo. Keep praying for and intentionally seek out a mentor; she'll pass on the baton of wisdom, faith, and life experience to you.

Are you running with the baton but not done with your lap yet? You have a mentor, and maybe you love the idea of mentoring someone else, but you're worried about fumbling the baton. After all, you're still figuring out what it means to be an adult and lean into growth. Be patient with yourself and don't rush too quickly to *do*. God is at work, and the day will come when you're ready to pass the baton. It doesn't have to be today. Remember, though, you don't have to be an expert or be perfect. You just have to be willing to be used by God.

Are you ready to pass on the baton of all you're learning from your mentor to the next runner? You want your life to be about more than just you. This may not look super organized and structured all the time. You may not even label it "mentoring" initially. But if you're stepping outside of yourself and stepping into another woman's life—taking time to care, to listen, to encourage, to share what God's taught you—that's passing on the baton.

Possibly this is what we've been missing all these years. We sit in an auditorium with a hundred other women, or in an arena with thousands, listening to the speaker talk about following Jesus. But then we go back to the real world, back to the struggle, the routine, the temptations, the fears, and doubts. Some of us press on alone, others stop running altogether. We sit down on the sidelines. We lose focus. We give up.

The only way to get across the finish line is together! Cheering each other on, crying together, celebrating together, sharing our stories, instilling hope, receiving new life, and fixing our eyes on Jesus until we get home.

LIVING IN THE "NOT YET"

Mentoring is not a one-semester college course or a thing you do for a year or two. It's a lifestyle of receiving and giving, of learning from each other. It's a paradigm shift from doing to becoming. There's a tension here—between who we are now and who we will be, the friction between the *now* and the *not yet*. Paul writes, "Dear friends, now we are children of God, and what we will be has not yet been made known" (1 John 3:2).

There will never come a time when you and I "arrive," when we stop growing and learning. Often, our daily reality is struggle. Mentoring won't make life easier per se. It can't protect you from life's hardships and difficulties, but it will give you new purpose and meaning in the midst of your struggles. A mentor can help you see where God is at work, even in the midst of our difficulties.

Just ask David. The prophet Samuel spoke truth over him, anointing him as the next king of Israel (1 Samuel 16:13). Samuel quickly became a mentor in David's life, someone he turned to for guidance and godly input. But when Samuel died years later (1 Samuel 25), David was still running for his life from King Saul, living in caves and sleeping with one eye open. Not exactly a happily ever after.

Where are You, God? I can't imagine the loneliness David faced. *Did I hear Samuel wrong, or did Samuel hear You wrong? Am I going crazy?*

What is the "not yet" you're struggling to walk out? It may be a struggle you chose, like spending time with God every day, learning to stand up to your boss, working out conflict in your relationship, figuring out how to parent, or deciding to move to a new town. Or it may be a struggle you're blindsided by, like losing your job, a painful breakup, or betrayal by a friend.

Living in the "not yet" can be pretty confusing sometimes. It's as if God says, "Here is the world. Beautiful and terrible things will happen. Don't be afraid. I am with you. Nothing can ever separate us."[2] God promises that He is always working for our good,[3] but He never promises we'll understand it in the moment. You and I and David can only see one sliver in time—this moment—but God sees the whole story of our lives. Our greatest struggles have the potential to shape our character profoundly, if we don't give up.

Though Samuel's part in David's story was over, God was still writing, dreaming, and planning. Jonathan, Nathan, and others were trusted confidants and mentors of his. David was far from perfect, too, and that gives me hope!

As king, David saw potential in unexpected places. He mentored his son Solomon, who was conceived after the king's sin of adultery and murder. And David reached out in love and support to Mephibosheth, who was Jonathan's crippled son.

Let's zoom out and see the big picture: Because of Hannah's faith in God, Samuel was born and dedicated to the Lord. Eli mentored Samuel. Samuel mentored David. David mentored Solomon. And Solomon mentored many people, including the Queen of Sheba, who came to know and believe in the one true God as a result. "Praise be to the Lord your God," she said, "who has delighted in you and placed you on the throne of Israel. Because of the Lord's eternal love for Israel, he has made you king to maintain justice and righteousness" (1 Kings 10:9).

This passing of the baton—God at work across four generations—is just a tiny snapshot. Our minds can't even begin to fully grasp the breadth and depth of the story God is writing. I doubt David had any grand revelations in the cave, but he clung to what he knew: *God is with me, God is for me, and somehow, I will get through this.* The irony of life is that we can rarely see God working in real time, only in hindsight.

In our own personal hiding-in-the-cave moments of life, we need to hear the truth. We need mentors and friends to shine light into the dark night of our souls and give us hope . . . because the story's not over yet!

BE THE CHANGE, LIVE DIFFERENTLY

Diana White was an ordinary eighteen-year-old. When she found out her friend Joni had been paralyzed in a diving accident, she showed up. More than making just a quick hospital visit, Diana went out of her way to keep showing up. She didn't offer cliché advice. But she committed to listen and encourage her, helping Joni see God in the midst of this tragedy. Joni reflects, "I just don't know what I would have done had God not provided Diana to me as a mentor . . . she was so key, so instrumental in my life, yet we were the same age."[3]

Joni could have easily given up hope. *My life is over!* She might have whined. *I'll never drive a car, no one will ever want to date me—I can't even feed myself!*

But because of one ordinary girl who showed up, listened, and spoke truth, Joni Eareckson Tada chose not to live as a victim of her paralysis. Instead, she turned it into her message, now speaking to audiences of thousands around the world: "When loneliness settles over your spirit like a lead apron, when pain and grief and anxiety conspire to push you to the edge of despair, remember God's mighty deeds in your life. Remember his kindness. . . . Suffering provides the gym equipment on which our faith can be exercised."[4]

Joni is passing on the baton of faith—the baton she first grappled with as she sat in that hospital bed and talked with Diana, reeling from the news of being paralyzed. It's hard to even quantify the full impact of Diana pointing Joni back to Jesus. And the most unique part of all? Diana and Joni were classmates. Sometimes, mentoring shows up where you least expect it.

The American dream focuses on getting, but mentoring is about giving yourself away—your time, your energy, your passion—so that others can grow and thrive. I encourage you, don't settle for a small life focused solely on money and stuff. And "[d]on't let anyone look down on you because you are young, but set an example for the believers in speech, in conduct, in love, in faith and in purity" (1 Timothy 4:12). It's never too early to build God's kingdom by mentoring others—Diana was just eighteen!

God has already gone in front of you, paving the way for where He wants to use you. So don't rush to mentor someone else. Don't get ahead of God. Just open your eyes. Look. Listen. Notice. Who is God bringing across your path? How can you pour your life into them?

LET'S DO THIS!

So much in our culture pushes us toward competing and comparing, but God's dream is this: women encouraging and building up other women. Rachel Held Evans reflects, "Following Jesus is a group activity, something we're supposed to do

together. We might not always do it within the walls of church
. . . but we're going to need each other."[5]

The church tells us to give our tithe, but I believe God
asks for even more. The ultimate gift of mentoring isn't giving
money—it's giving yourself, giving your life away in a thousand
different ways, big or small. Giving your life to create new life
. . . through Jesus in you. Mentoring is an investment that will
outlast you and live on long after you are gone.

We all want to do something great for God, but could it
be that our ordinary acts of loving, serving, listening, caring,
and giving of ourselves are what really create change? "It is you.
It is me. The kingdom advances in our small neighborhoods
and small acts of love and small moments of faithfulness and
small feats of courage," Jen Hatmaker challenges us. "It is not
encapsulated in programs and top-down structures but activat-
ed through the body of Christ daring to be faithful everywhere
we've been planted."[6]

The church is often about big gatherings, thinking that
numbers mean growth. But change could be as simple as this:
find a woman further along in her walk with the Lord to pour
into you and shape you, and find a younger woman that you can
invest in.

I say we stop joining the crowd of whiners who vent on
social media about everything that's wrong in our world. Let's
stop tearing other women down just to feel better about ourselves. And let's stop huddling in our caves feeling alone and sad.

Let's start a movement. Let's commit together to *be there* for
each other as women—not just in theory, but in the messy and
painful and wonderful moments of life.

Let's build a culture of supporting and nurturing and loving and celebrating each woman's uniqueness. Let's listen and encourage and empower and speak life.

Let's stop gossiping and start calling out the potential that we see in our friends and coworkers. We are not in a competition; we're comrades journeying together.

Let's give not just our money, but ourselves away. Let's be the change we want to see in our world, linking arms across cities and states and continents and generations.

You see, this journey to becoming the woman God created you to be doesn't end here. It's only just beginning. God is turning your page . . . putting His pen to the paper as He writes the next chapter in your story. You've met many of my friends through these pages, and listened as they've wrestled and explored and discovered and grown.

Now it's your turn. Step out. Challenge yourself. Go after the dreams God has put in your heart. Seek wise counsel. Surround yourself with women you can learn from. Give yourself away. And even as you do, hold loosely to your dreams and tightly to your heavenly Father. Remember, you can be "confident of this, that he who began a good work in you will carry it on to completion until the day of Christ Jesus" (Philippians 1:6).

When we meet face-to-face, and our race is done, I can't wait to hear your story. But until that day, be brave. Be yourself. And know that you never have to walk alone.

Respond

1. Who has poured into your life? What mark have they left? Take a moment to thank God for these people. How can you communicate your gratitude to them?

2. Where are you today? Pick one of the following and share why:

   • I'm trying to run a marathon, doing my race solo.

   • I'm in the middle of my lap in the relay and wondering if I will finish.

   • I'm excited to pass on the baton, but I need God's help.

3. What does this mean for you as you continue to walk out the journey of mentoring? Who is God bringing across your path to love and serve? Talk with God about your next step.

About the Author

Jayme Hull is an author, Christian communicator, and ministry leader, encouraging and motivating audiences to invest in mentoring and grow in their faith. Through her unique stories and passionate heart for Christ, women are refreshed to live an authentic faith that is the "real deal." Encountering Christ as a college student at New York University, Jayme quickly realized she was ill-equipped to journey alone, and reached out for mentorship and community from Christian women further down the path. Shaped by countless mentors over the past thirty-five years, Jayme now has the incredible privilege of sitting every week with millennial women, roughly twenty-five to thirty-five, who are wrestling to live from a place of authenticity and wholeness. Through her devotionals, blogging, training, speaking, and mentoring, Jayme has no greater joy than to pour into women's lives—whether over a cup of coffee or through the written word.

Jayme resides in Franklin, Tennessee, with her husband, John. They have three married children and are the proud grandparents of four grandchildren.

You can connect with her at these places:

Sign up to receive Jayme's blog at
www.JaymeLeeHull.com

Follow Jayme on Facebook,
www.facebook.comJaymeHullFaceToFaceMentoring

On Twitter,
www.twitter.com/JaymeHull

Jayme is available for consulting and speaking at your events on mentoring and reaching out to the millennial generation.

Laura Captari is a counselor, author and lover of stories. She cowrote *Face to Face*, *Be Rebellious*, and *Orphan Justice*. Laura is a doctoral student at the University of North Texas.

Notes

Chapter 1: Invitation to a Journey

1. Kate Harris, *Wonder Women: Navigating the Challenges of Motherhood, Career, and Identity, Barna Group Frames* (Grand Rapids, MI: Zondervan, 2013), 48.

Chapter 2: The Influence of a Mentor

1. Henry Blackaby and Claude King, *Experiencing God: Knowing and Doing the Will of God* (Nashville, TN: B&H Publishing, 2004), 29.
2. Ibid., 30.
3. Ibid.
4. Henry Blackaby, Richard Blackaby, and Claude King, *Experiencing God: Knowing and Doing the Will of God, Revised Edition* (Nashville, TN: B&H Publishing, 2008), 151.

Chapter 3: Messy Faith

1. Anne Lamott, *Bird by Bird: Some Instructions on Writing and Life* (New York: Random House, 1995), 28; *Plan B: Further Thoughts on Faith* (New York: Penguin Group, 2005), 257.
2. Data gathered by the U.S. Census Bureau, David Bancroft Avrick, "How Many People Move Each Year—and Who Are They?" Melissadata.com, accessed July 28, 2015, http://www.melissadata.com/enews/articles/0705b/1.htm
3. Harris, *Wonder Women*, 62.
4. Brandon Cox, *Rewired: How Using Today's Technology Can Bring You Back to Deeper Relationships, Real Conversations, and the Age-Old Methods of Sharing God's Love* (Lake Mary, FL: Charisma House, 2014), 35.
5. Rainer Maria Rilke, *Letters to a Young Poet* (Mineola, NY: Dover Publications, 2002), 21.
6. Criss Jami, *Killosophy: Killing Knowledge, Loving Wisdom* (Charleston, SC: CreateSpace Independent Publishing, 2015), 98.

Chapter 4: Living on Purpose: How to Find a Mentor

1. Andy Stanley, *Visioneering: God's Blueprint for Developing and Maintaining Personal Vision* (Colorado Springs, CO: Multnomah, 1999), 45.
2. John Ortberg, *If You Want to Walk on Water, You've Got to Get Out of the Boat* (Grand Rapids, MI: Zondervan, 2001), 94.
3. Jen Pollock Michel, "How to Find Your Calling," *Practicing Faith*, June 1, 2015, http://practicingfaith.com/how-to-find-your-calling/

4. Fredrick Buechner, *Wishful Thinking: A Seeker's ABC* (Woonsocket, RI: Mowbray, 1994), 95.
5. Ann Voskamp, "How the Hidden Dangers of Comparison are Killing Us (And Our Daughters): The Measuring Stick Principle," Aholyexperience .com, November 6, 2013, http://www.aholyexperience.com/2013/11/ how-the-hidden-dangers-of-comparison-are-killing-us-and-our-daughters-the-measuring-stick-principle/

Chapter 5: The Courage to Step Out

1. Ortberg, *If You Want to Walk on Water, You've Got to Get Out of the Boat*, 98.
2. Nicole Williams, "Infographic: Women and Mentoring in the US," Blog, linkedin.com, October 25, 2011, http://blog.linkedin .com/2011/10/25/mentoring-women/
3. Ibid.
4. Bill Hybels, *Just Walk Across the Room: Simple Steps Pointing People to Faith* (Grand Rapids, MI: Zondervan, 2006), 72.
5. http://www.goodreads.com/quotes/tag/risk-taking

Chapter 6: Popping the Question with Confidence

1. Ellen Goodman, "Ellen Goodman Quotes," Goodreads.com, accessed July 28, 2015, http://www.goodreads.com/quotes/694993-we-spend-january-1st-walking-through-our-lives-room-by
2. As cited in Lisa Bevere, *Nurture: Give and Get What You Need to Flourish* (New York: Hachette Book Group, 2008), 13.
3. Susan Hunt, *Spiritual Mothering: The Titus 2 Model for Women Mentoring Women* (Wheaton, IL: Crossway, 1992), 12.
4. John Schlimm, "10 Ways a Mentor Can Change Your Life," John-schlimm.com, April 23, 2015, http://johnschlimm.com/2015/04/23/10-ways-a-mentor-can-change-your-life/

Chapter 7: I Have a Mentor . . . Now What?

1. "One to One," Apple.com, accessed July 28, 2015, https://www.apple .com/retail/learn/one-to-one/
2. Ancient Chinese proverb

Chapter 8: Navigating Conflict

1. Max Lucado, *When God Whispers Your Name* (Nashville, TN: Thomas Nelson, 1999), 44.
2. Dr. Julie Gottman as cited in "The Art and Science of Love—15 Favorite Moments from Our Gottman Workshop Weekend," Staymar-riedblog.com, December 9, 2014, http://staymarriedblog.com/the-art-science-of-love-15-favorite-moments-staymarried/

3. http://segal-law.com/practice-areas/train-derailments/

4. Gary Thomas, *Sacred Marriage: What if God Designed Marriage to Make Us Holy More Than to Make Us Happy* (Grand Rapids, MI: Zondervan, 2000), 129.

Chapter 9: Balance in a Crazy World

1. Harris, *Wonder Women*, 33.

2. Lysa TerKeurst, *The Best Yes: Making Wise Decisions in the Midst of Endless Demands* (Nashville, TN: Thomas Nelson, 2014), 5.

3. Sarah Bessey, *Jesus Feminist: God's Radical Notion That Women are People, Too* (New York: Howard Books, 2013), 114.

Chapter 10: Moving Forward

1. Henri J. M. Nouwen, *Life of the Beloved: Spiritual Living in a Secular World* (New York: Crossroad Publishing, 2002), 10.

2. Heather Holleman, *Seated with Christ: Living Freely in a Culture of Comparison* (Chicago: Moody, 2015), 103.

3. Nouwen, *Life of the Beloved*, 10, 32.

4. Beth Moore, *So Long, Insecurity: You've Been a Bad Friend to Us* (Carol Stream, IL: Tyndale, 2010), 15.

Chapter 11: In Search of Romeo

1. D'vera Cohn, Jeffrey Passel, Wendy Wang, and Gretchen Livingston, "Barely Half of U.S. Adults are Married—a Record Low," Pew Research Center, December 14, 2011, http://www.pewsocialtrends .org/2011/12/14/barely-half-of-u-s-adults-are-married-a-record-low/

2. Elisabeth Elliot, *Loneliness* (Nashville, TN: Nelson, 1988), 33–39.

3. As cited in Elisabeth Elliot, *Through Gates of Splendor* (Carol Stream, IL: Tyndale, 1981), 20.

4. Amanda Bast, "26, Unmarried, and Childless," *Converge Magazine*, September 9, 2013, http://convergemagazine.com/26-unmarried-and-childless-8736/

5. Annie F. Downs, "What More Do You Want?: How Can We Be Content in Any Stage of Life?" (presentation, Q Women Conference, Nashville, TN, November 3, 2014).

Chapter 12: Getting Unstuck

1. Sanctus Real, "Whatever You're Doing (Something Heavenly)," by Dan Gartley, Matt Hammitt. Mark Graalman, Chris Rohman, and Pete Prevost, in *We Need Each Other*, Birdwing Music, River Oaks Music Company, Stonebrook Music Company, February 12, 2008.

2. Ellery Sadler, "The Art of Holding Loosely," *Relevant Magazine*, May 11, 2015, http://www.relevantmagazine.com/life/art-holding-loosely.

3. Bethany Hamilton, "Bethany Hamilton Quotes," Goodreads.com, accessed July 28, 2015, http://www.goodreads.com/quotes/1270897-

courage-doesn-t-mean-you-don-t-get-afraid-courage-means-you

4. Stasi Eldredge, *Becoming Myself: Embracing God's Dream for You* (Colorado Springs, CO: David C Cook, 2013), 121–22.

Section Five: Pass It On

1. Mother Teresa, *No Greater Love* (Novato, CA: New World Library, 2001), 29.
2. Buechner, *Wishful Thinking: A Seeker's ABC*, 34.
3. Joni Eareckson Tada, "Be a Mentor," Joni and Friends Radio, April 13, 2011, http://www.joniandfriends.org/radio/5-minute/be-mentor/
4. Joni Eareckson Tada, *A Lifetime of Wisdom: Embracing the Way God Heals You* (Grand Rapids, MI: Zondervan, 2009), 63; Joni Eareckson Tada, *Making Sense of Suffering* (Carson, CA: Rose Publishing, 2012), 10.
5. Rachel Held Evans, *Searching for Sunday: Loving, Leaving, and Finding the Church* (Nashville, TN: Thomas Nelson, 2015), 255.
6. Jen Hatmaker, *Interrupted: When Jesus Wrecks Your Comfortable Christianity, Revised and Expanded* (Carol Stream, IL: NavPress, 2014), 176.

My Standing Ovation

*"Every time I think of you, I give
thanks to my God. Whenever I pray,
I make my requests for all of you with joy,
for you have been my partners in spreading
the good news about Christ from the time
you first heard it until now."*

PHILIPPIANS 1:3–5 NLT

Authoring this book has been like attending a fabulous Broadway musical: The audience is impressed with the production from scene to scene—the costume changes, sets, lighting, and beautiful music. What they don't see, however, is the countless hours spent creating the set, the committed back-stage crews, the expert makeup artists . . . and the list goes on. Each of these people is key to making the show a success. And the same is true for this book!

These acknowledgments are my standing ovation of deep appreciation for each person who has been a gift from God along this writing journey. Picture me (I know you can!) standing, energetically clapping, and cheering loudly with every ounce of my being: BRAVO!

First of all, my deepest thanks to my Savior, the divine mentor. Without Jesus, this book would never have been possible. The Lord has directed every step of this book and I'm grateful to have this opportunity to share my God story. It is my prayer for the Holy Spirit to move through these words to help women of all ages connect with God and each other in fresh and meaningful ways.

Words fall short to express my gratitude for my incredible husband, John, and my family, Joanna, Skylar, Jason, Sarah, Sutton, Jered, Lauren, Gabriela, and Piper. You have been my cheerleaders and encouragers every step of the way. I love you with all of my heart and soul.

I want to thank my mentors, many of whom are mentioned throughout these pages. I am who I am today because these women chose to pour into my life and help me grow in my faith. And to the women I have been privileged to mentor over the years: I love you. Each and every one of you has been an inspiration in my life. I have no greater joy than to pass on the baton of mentoring to others and see the world changed one heart and life at a time.

To my talented and exceptional coauthor and friend, Laura Captari: I'm forever grateful to God for bringing us together to write this book. You and I have witnessed the hand of God from the first day we met, and it has been an amazing unforgettable journey writing together. You're the best! You have captured my passion for mentoring, and this book would never exist in its current form without your help. Also, many thanks to Shawn Kuhn for introducing us.

Natalie Mills, acquisitions editor at Moody Collective, thank you for catching the vision of mentoring and believing in this project. Without your enthusiastic support, inspiration, and guidance, this book would not have been possible. My sincere thanks also goes to Judy Dunagan, Pam Pugh, and the entire team at Moody for walking me through the editing process.

To Richard Blackaby: Thank you for spending the time to pray over me during our conversations within the Blackaby Coaching Certification. I felt the Holy Spirit move and knew God was blessing my next step . . . even though I didn't know it would be this book. God knew! Many thanks to my spiritual leadership coaches Bob Royall and Brett Pyle for their godly advice and counsel along the way. Credit also goes to several writing and speaking coaches. Each of you saw my potential and believed in me when I didn't believe in myself. My deepest thanks to Kathy Carlton Willis, Vonda Skelton, Carolyn Knefely, and Shannon Ethridge.

I am eternally grateful to my parents, Patsy and Clyde, now resting in eternal peace, for their investment in me, and I share the joy and celebration of this book with my sisters, SuAnne Wolff and Sandy Herrmann, and their families. Thanks for all of your support.

My love and thanks to the many friends who read drafts, attended focus groups, gave feedback, and sent encouraging words along the way: Lindey Newton, Emily Mitchell, Jordan Cleveland, Emily Maugans, Susan Browne, Angie Lester, Hannah Strickland, Aly Chase, Cheryl Maier, Mari-Lee Ruddy, Toni Staub, John Stiles, Kayleigh Avery, Ashleigh Whitehorn, Priscilla Babrick, Brittanny White, Caroline Webb, and Bucky Rosenbaum.

And to the powerful prayer warriors who stood on the front lines for me: Leslie Williams, Lorie Marsh, Medora Strickland,

Brenda Wilkerson, Joy Gartzke, Connie Keller, Cybil Murray, Natalie Hemby, Anne Kerr, Donna Jones, Amy Cordell, Margaret Kimbrough, and all my dear friends at Judson Baptist Church Women's Ministry, Matthew Page, Amy Bryant, and all the mentors at The Church at Avenue South, Nashville.

Finally, I'm deeply grateful for my pastor, Aaron Bryant, at The Church at Avenue South, Nashville. Thank you for sharing in my passion to mentor millennials. I can't wait to see the kingdom men and women God raises up through the mentoring program there!

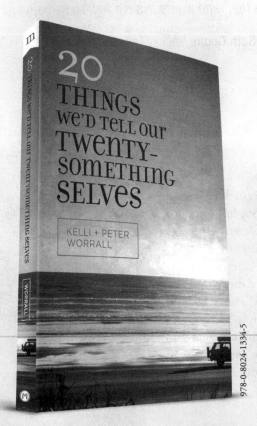

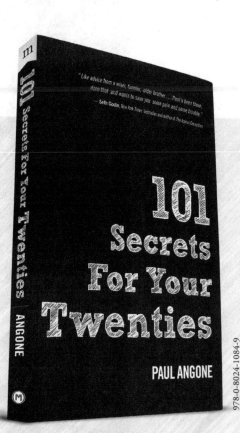

RADICAL

WITH DAVID PLATT

Radical with David Platt, a half-hour national teaching program, airs daily on Moody Radio. Bestselling author, sought-after conference speaker, and pastor, David Platt brings to each program solid, passionate Bible teaching aimed at equipping and mobilizing Christians to make disciples among the nations so that the Lord receives the glory due His name.

www.radicalwithdavidplatt.org

MOODY
Radio™

*From the Word **to Life***